海外藏中国艺术品
OVERSEAS CHINESE ART SELECTION

绘画卷·宋(上)

PAINTINGS · SONG (1)

本书编写组 编著
Compiled by Editorial Team

郭怀宇 本卷主编
Edited by Guo Huaiyu

NEWSTAR PRESS
新星出版社

图书在版编目（CIP）数据

海外藏中国艺术品．绘画卷．宋．上：汉英对照 / 郭怀宇主编；本书编写组编著．-- 北京：新星出版社，2024.12

ISBN 978-7-5133-5439-4

Ⅰ．①海… Ⅱ．①郭… ②本… Ⅲ．①中国画－中国－宋代－图录 Ⅳ．① K870.2

中国国家版本馆 CIP 数据核字 (2024) 第 056641 号

海外藏中国艺术品 绘画卷·宋（上）

本书编写组 编 著
郭 怀 宇 本卷主编

责任编辑 李文彧　　**特约编辑** 丁文文
英文审校 韩 华　　**责任校对** 刘 义
装帧设计 冷暖儿　　**责任印制** 李珊珊

出 版 人 马汝军
出版发行 新星出版社
（北京市西城区车公庄大街丙 3 号楼 8001　100044）
网　　址 www.newstarpress.com
法律顾问 北京市岳成律师事务所
印　　刷 河北尚唐印刷包装有限公司
开　　本 889mm × 1194mm　1/16
印　　张 13.75
字　　数 344 千字
版　　次 2024 年 12 月第 1 版　2024 年 12 月第 1 次印刷
书　　号 ISBN 978-7-5133-5439-4
定　　价 308.00 元

总机：010-88310888　传真：010-65270449　销售中心：010-88310811

出版说明

按中国文物学会统计，鸦片战争以来流失海外的中国文物超过一千万件。这些文物是中国文物重要而特殊的组成部分，除其历史、文化、艺术等方面价值，更因其所凝结的民族情感而备受各界关注。

近年来，中国政府积极推动文物追索，国内外学界也涌现出一批新的研究成果，文物流失研究方兴未艾。但受诸多因素限制，海外文物归国面临着许多实际困难，能追回的仍只是很少一部分。在此情况下，加强中外合作、开展联合研究，通过出版、数字化等方式让更多人有机会了解相关资料和研究成果，成了推动流失文物"活起来"、促进中华文化海外传播的一条可行路径。在国内外专家学者、文博机构等的支持下，新星出版社推出这套《海外藏中国艺术品》，希望能为广大读者及学者提供一套可资观赏、查阅和研究的参考读物。

《海外藏中国艺术品》出版之际，我们尤其希望通过这套书向林树中先生致敬。林树中先生自20世纪80年代起，花费近20年时间，自费走遍40多个国家和地区的200多所博物馆，呕心沥血、锲而不舍，记录了大量海外藏中国文物资料，编纂出版了《海外藏中国历代名画》，成为这一领域具有重大影响力的开创性成果。2013年，新星出版社联手林树中教授共同策划了《海外藏中国艺术品》项目，旨在全面整理他对流失海外的绘画、雕塑、书法、工艺品的丰富记录和研究成果。不幸的是，筹备工作开始不久，林树中教授因病辞世，这给整理与编纂工作带来巨大挑战，出版计划也因此被迫中断。

《海外藏中国艺术品》编纂出版的两大关键因素是专家学者的专业把关和海外藏品的图片授权。在重启并继续推动项目的过程中，我们重新组建了国内外专家组成的编纂团队，英国独角兽公司则协调许多知名博物馆向我们开放图片授权。合法取得文物图片使用授权后，编纂团队对入选文物加以鉴别与甄选，按时代顺序进行分卷、编排，并对文物中英文定名、创作时代、创作者、材质、规格等馆藏信息进行逐一确认。

《海外藏中国艺术品》共计20卷，收录文物2279件，来自海外33家知名博物馆，涵盖了铜器（2册）、陶瓷（3册）、书法（3册）、绘画（11册）和造像（1册）五大门类。

此次出版的《海外藏中国艺术品》因故未能收录金银器、玉器、服饰等艺术门类。我们愿以《海外藏中国艺术品》的出版为契机，努力搭建研究交流和成果出版发布平台，期待与国内外有关各方携手，共同推进流失文物领域相关工作，为中华优秀传统文化传承发展和中华文化国际传播作出新贡献。

囿于出版者水平，书中难免缺漏错讹之处，敬请专家、读者指正。

Preface

According to statistics from the Chinese Society of Cultural Relics, over ten million Chinese cultural relics have been dispersed overseas since the Opium War in the mid-19th century. They represent an important and unique part of China's cultural heritage. Beyond their historical, cultural, and artistic value, they are also of great interest to all sectors of society due to the national sentiments they embody.

In recent years, the Chinese government has been actively engaging in the recovery of Chinese cultural relics, and domestic and international academia has seen a surge in new research, making the study of the loss of Chinese cultural relics a burgeoning field. However, practical challenges have constrained the repatriation efforts, resulting in the recovery of only a small fraction of these relics. In light of this, it has become a feasible approach to enhance visibility and awareness of these artifacts through strengthened international cooperation, joint research, and the dissemination of materials and findings via publications and digitalization. With the support of domestic and international experts, scholars, cultural institutions, and museums, New Star Press has published the *Overseas Chinese Art Selection* series. This series aims to provide reference materials for readers and scholars to appreciate, consult, and study.

Upon the publication of this series, we would like to take this opportunity to pay tribute to Mr. Lin Shuzhong. Beginning in the 1980s, Lin devoted nearly two decades visiting over 200 museums in more than 40 countries and regions at his own expense. With remarkable dedication and perseverance, he documented a vast amount of information about Chinese cultural relics overseas and compiled and published *Famous Chinese Paintings Abroad*, which has become a groundbreaking work with significant influence in this field. In 2013, New Star Press collaborated with Professor Lin on *Overseas Chinese Art Selection*, aiming to comprehensively organize his extensive records and research on paintings, sculptures, calligraphy, and crafts lost overseas. Tragically, shortly after the preparatory work began, he passed away due to illness, presenting significant challenges to the project's continuation. As a result, the publication plan had to be suspended.

The successful compilation and publication of *Overseas Chinese Art Selection* depended on two critical factors: the professional scrutiny of experts and scholars and the license to use images granted by overseas museums. In the process of restarting the project, we set up a new compilation team composed of local and international experts. UK-based Unicorn Publishing Group LLP coordinated with many renowned overseas museums to secure permissions for image use. After legally obtaining their permissions, the compilation team appraised and selected artifacts, organized them into different categories and in chronological order, and confirmed collection information for each piece, including Chinese and English names, the time of creation, the artist's name, material, specifications, and other relevant information.

Overseas Chinese Art Selection consists of 20 volumes, with 2,279 cultural relics from 33 renowned museums overseas, covering five major categories: bronzes (two volumes), ceramics (three volumes), calligraphy (three volumes), paintings (11 volumes), and sculptures (one volume).

Categories such as gold and silver wares, jade wares, and costumes are not included. We hope this publication will help build a platform for research exchanges and publication of research findings. We are looking forward to working together with partners at home and abroad to jointly pursue initiatives related to lost Chinese cultural treasures, and contribute to the inheritance and development of China's excellent traditional culture and a wider knowledge of Chinese culture globally.

Despite our best efforts, errors and inaccuracies may be present due to the limitations of the publisher's expertise. We kindly invite experts and readers to point them out for further improvement.

凡例

一、《海外藏中国艺术品》绘画卷收录了宋、元、明、清代共1178件画作，每件画作由图片和中英文基本信息两部分组成。

二、本卷中画作依照时代分册：宋代2册，元代1册，明、清代各4册，共计11册。

三、本卷中具体画作顺序基本依照画家生卒年先后编排，同时兼顾风格、流派等相关因素。同一画家的画作如有准确年款，则依年款先后编排，无准确年款的画作基本按立轴、手卷、册页、扇面形制依序编排；传为某画家的画作，均编排在该画家画作最后。佚名画作均编排于各时代最后，并依人物、山水、花鸟等门类略作分类。

四、本卷中已有中文定名的画作名称，与官网名称不一致的，均依已有中文定名。

五、本卷中以朝代标明画作的时代信息，其相应的英文表述，统一注明朝代和具体起止时间，如“Ming dynasty (1368—1644)”。部分画作有准确年款，均注明。

六、本卷中画作的材质基本统一为纸本水墨、纸本设色、绢本水墨、绢本设色、绫本水墨、绫本设色六种，对应英文为ink on paper，ink and color on paper，ink on silk，ink and color on silk，ink on satin，ink and color on satin。将ink and touches of color on silk；ink，color，gold and silver on silk；ink and color on gold-flecked paper；ink and pale color on paper等统一为以上相应材质。

七、本卷中画作的尺寸基本为画面尺寸，并注明了画面纵、横尺寸，对应英文为H、W。

八、本卷充分尊重各海外博物馆的要求，将每幅画作的出处和图片版权信息均详细列出。但因该信息并非对画作本身的描述，故未翻译成中文。其中个别博物馆或美术馆，如大阪市立美术馆，未提供该信息，因此未收录。

Guide to the Reader

i. The paintings volume of *Overseas Chinese Art Selection* contains 1178 pieces of paintings from the Song (960-1279), Yuan (1271-1368), Ming (1368-1644) and Qing (1644-1911) dynasties. Each piece is accompanied by basic information in Chinese and English.

ii. The paintings are presented chronologically in eleven volumes, of which two volumes are for paintings from Song Dynasty, one volume including those of Yuan Dynasty, four volumes for those of Ming Dynasty and another four for paintings from Qing Dynasty.

iii. The order of the paintings within each dynasty generally follows the period of time when the artists lived, taking the artistic styles, genres, etc. into consideration. Paintings by the same artist are primarily sorted in accordance with the exact chronology information when known; otherwise, they are arranged in accordance with the form of the paintings, namely in the order of handing scroll, handscroll, album leaf, fan paintings. Paintings attributed to an uncertain artist, are placed at the very end of the composer's paintings. Anonymous paintings are sorted at the end of paintings of each dynasty in this volume in accordance with the category of figure, scenery, birds and flowers, etc.

iv. The established Chinese names of those paintings which may be given different names by the official website will be retained in this volume.

v. The era of the paintings is marked by the dynasty in the volume. Both the dynasty and specific starting and ending years of the dynasties are indicated in the English description, such as "Ming Dynasty (1368-1644)". The specific creating time of some paintings is already known, which has been presented clearly.

vi. The materials used in the paintings in this volume are primarily summarized into six types: namely ink on paper, ink and color on paper, ink on silk, ink and color on silk, ink on stain, ink and color on stain. While there are numerous varitions, such as ink and touches of color on silk; ink, color, gold and silver on silk; ink and color on gold-flecked paper; ink and pale color on paper; etc. These have been standardized to the above categories for consistency.

vii. Dimensions in the basic information of this volume primarily represent the size of the painting's image, with vertical measurements denoted by 'H' and horizontal measurements by 'W'.

viii. This volume fully respects the requirements of overseas museums, the credit line and image copyright of paintings provided by the museums have been listed in details. However, since such information is not a description of the paintings themselves, it is presented only in English. Some museums or galleries, such as The Osaka City Museum of Fine Arts, do not provide those information of the paintings when displaying them, therefore such information of some paintings is omitted here.

目 录
CONTENTS

宋（上）
The Song Dynasty（1）

1. 女史箴图 003
Admonitions Scroll

2. 洛神赋图 007
Nymph of Luo River

3. 照夜白图 011
Night-shining White

4. 圉人呈马图.. 015
Horse and Groom

5. 五星二十八宿神形图 019
Five Planets and Twenty-eight Constellations

6. 送子天王图 023
Legendary Story of Siddhartha's Birth

7. 伏生授经图 027
Fu Sheng Expounding Classic

8. 明皇避暑宫图.................................... 028
Summer Palace of Emperor Ming Huang

9. 宫中图 031
In Palace

10. 宫中图... 033
In Palace

11. 琉璃堂人物图 035
Scholars of Liuli Hall

12. 内人双陆图.. 039
Palace Ladies Playing Back Gammon

13. 二祖调心图.. 043
Two Patriarchs Harmonizing Their Minds

14. 竹虫图... 044
Insects and Bamboos

15. 溪岸图... 045
Riverbank

16. 溪山兰若图.. 046
Buddhist Retreat by Stream and Mountains

17. 寒林策驴图.. 047
Travelers in Wintry Forest

18. 读碑窠石图.. 048
Reading Memorial Stele

19. 江山楼观图.. 051
Landscape with Pavilions

20. 江村图... 053
River Hamlet

21. 夏山图... 055
Summer Mountains

22. 雪山楼阁图.. 057
Winter Landscape with Temples

23. 树色平远图.. 059
Old Trees, Level Distance

24. 晚霭图... 063
Rosy Sunset

25. 孝经图... 067
Classic of Filial Piety

26. 醉僧图... 077
Drunken Monk

27. 潇湘卧游图.. 081
Imaginary Tour Through Xiao Xiang Region

28. 竹禽图... 087
Finches and Bamboo

29. 五色鹦鹉图.. 091
Five-colored Parakeet

30. 捣练图... 095
Court Ladies Preparing Newly Woven Silk

31. 荔枝禽鸟图.. 098
Bunch of Purple Lychees

32. 冬景山水图 099
Winter Evening Landscape

33. 获鹿图 101
Stag Hunt

34. 蕃王礼佛图 105
Barbarian Royalty Worshiping Buddha

35. 藻鱼图 108
Fish at Play

36. 睢阳五老图之朱贯像 109
Portrait of Zhu Guan from Set Five Old Men of Suiyang

37. 睢阳五老图之杜衍像 110
Portrait of Du Yan from Set Five Old Men of Suiyang

38. 睢阳五老图之毕世长像 111
Portrait of Bi Shichang from Set Five Old Men of Suiyang

39. 睢阳五老图之王涣像 112
Portrait of Wang Huan from Set Five Old Men of Suiyang

40. 睢阳五老图之冯平像 113
Portrait of Feng Ping from Set Five Old Men of Suiyang

41. 乞巧图 114
Palace Banquet

42. 聘金图 117
Diplomatic Mission to Jin

43. 风雪松杉图 119
Wind and Snow in Fir Pines

44. 明妃出塞图 123
Empress Mingfei Crossing Border

45. 平林霁色图 125
Clear Weather in Valley

46. 雪中林鸟图 127
Birds in Grove in Mountainous Winter Landscape

47. 晋文公复国图 129
Duke Wen of Jin Recovering His State

48. 远岫晴云图 133
Clouds on Clear Day Around Distant Peaks

49. 云山图 135
Cloudy Mountains

50. 云山图 139
Cloudy Mountains

51. 云木夏寒图 141
Cloudy Woods, Summer Chill

52. 婴戏图 144
Children Playing with Balance Toy

53. 货郎婴戏图 145
Knickknack Peddler

54. 红白芙蓉图 147
Red and White Hibiscuses

55. 古木竹禽图 149
Birds on Tree above Cataract

56. 竹虫图 150
Bamboo and Insects

57. 仿高克明溪山雪意图 153
Streams and Mountains Under Fresh Snow After Gao Keming

58. 听琴图 154
Listening to Qin

59. 洞山渡水图 155
Priest Dongshan Wading Stream

60. 寒江独钓图 156
Solitary Angler on Wintery River

61. 水溪竹禽图 157
Bamboo and Ducks by Rushing Stream

62. 高士观瀑图 158
Scholar Viewing Waterfall

63. 举杯邀月图 159
Drinking in Moonlight

64. 松溪观鹿图 160
Watching Deer by Pine Shaded Stream

65. 月下观梅图 161
Viewing Plum Blossoms by Moonlight

66. 松荫玩月图 162
Viewing Moon Under Pine Tree

67. 古松楼阁图 163
Old Pine and Pavilion

68. 溪山烟霭图 164
Evening Mist over Valley

69. 烟村秋霭图 165
Cottages in Misty Grove in Autumn

70. 潇湘八景图 167
Eight Views of Xiaoxiang Rivers

71. 货郎图 182
Knickknack Peddler

72. 诗经·豳风·七月图 185
Illustrations of "Seventh Month" from Odes of Bin

73. 诗经·豳风·七月图 189
Illustrations of "Seventh Month" from Odes of Bin

74. 诗经·豳风·七月图 193
Illustrations of "Seventh Month" from Odes of Bin

75. 诗经·小雅·鸿雁图 199
Illustrations of "Wild Geese" from Odes of Bin

76. 秋郊牧牛图 202
Buffalo and Boy in Autumnal Landscape

77. 松壑隐栖图 203
Hermitage by Pine-covered Bluff

版权支持 205
Image Contributors

编辑、出版人员 207
Editorial Staff

宋（上）

The Song Dynasty (I)

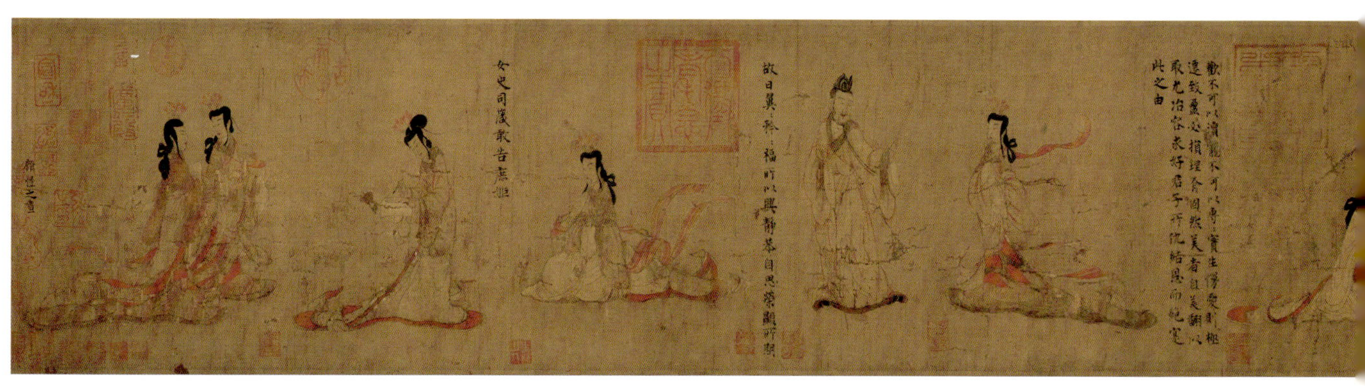

不能到此卷也
史箴圖流傳千
數百餘年而神
采煥發意態如
生非後人窺測
所可涯涘董香
光跋李伯時瀟
湘圖云顧中舍
所藏名卷有四
以此為第一信哉
是圖向貯御書
房繼得李畫蜀
江九歌瀟湘諸
卷適符董跋中
名卷之數為移
置建福宮之靜
怡軒額曰四美之
以志秘賞千古
法寶不引而會
正復不可思議
率紀數言亦為
是卷慶劍合也
乾隆丙寅夏至
前五日靜怡軒
御筆

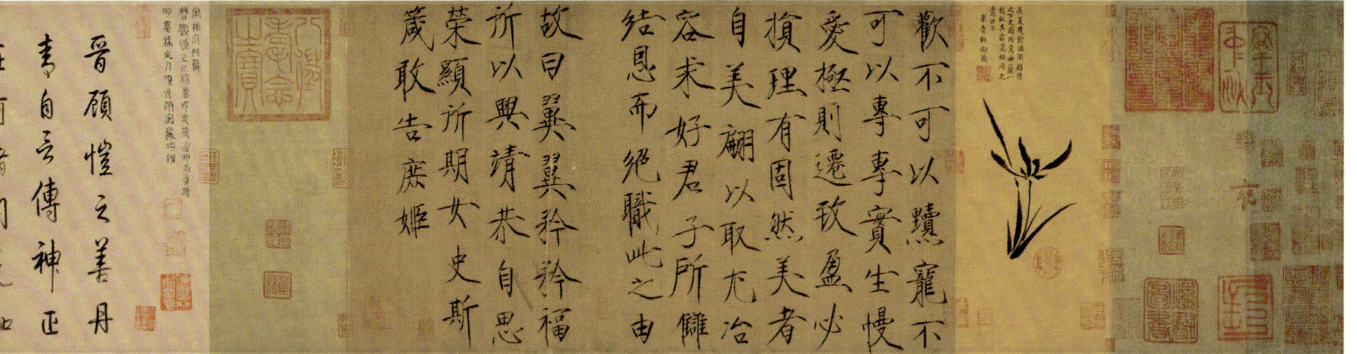

1. 女史箴图

宋或以前
（传）顾恺之
绢本设色
手卷
纵24.37、横343.75厘米
不列颠博物馆

Admonitions Scroll

Song dynasty (960–1279) or earlier
Attributed to Gu Kaizhi
Ink and color on silk
Handscroll
H×W: 24.37×343.75 cm
The British Museum
Purchased from:Capt. C. Johnson

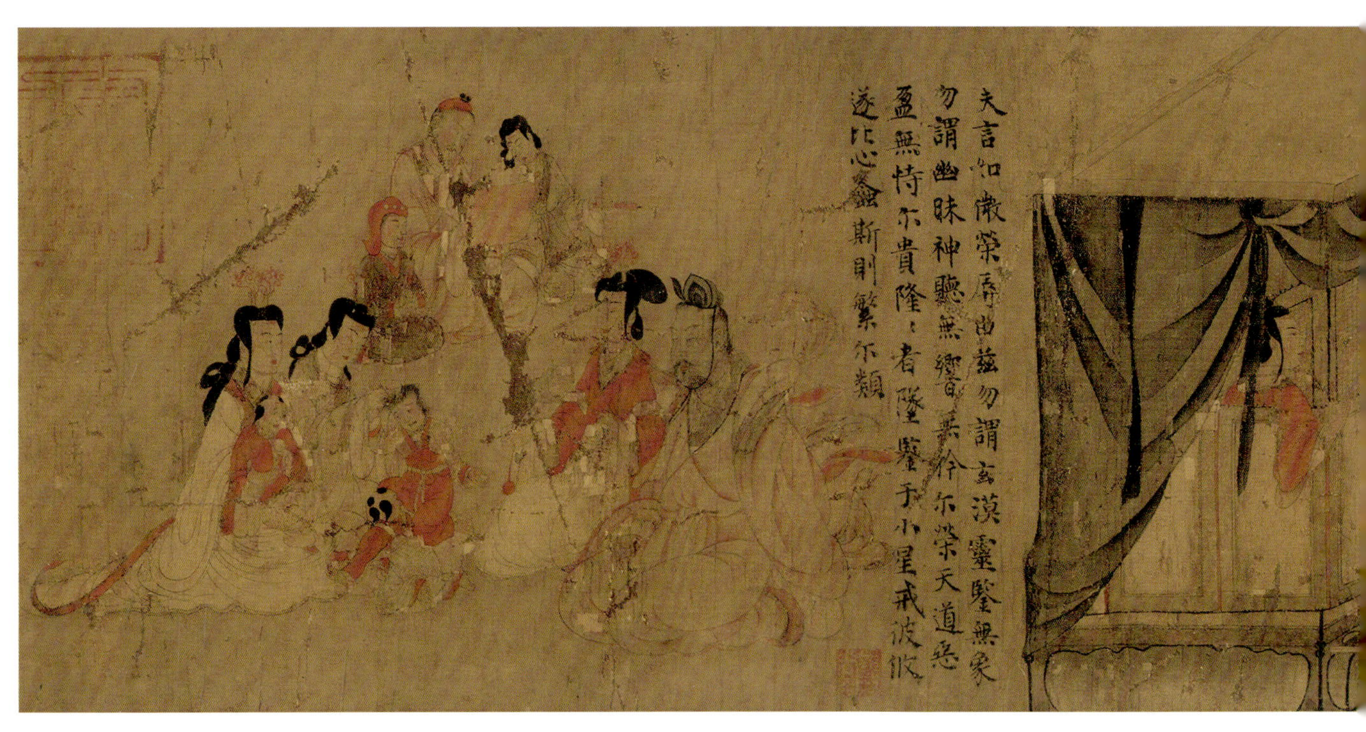
夫言如微榮辱由茲勿謂玄漠靈鑒無象
勿謂幽昧神聽無響無矜爾榮天道惡
盈無恃爾貴隆隆者墜鑒于小星戒彼攸
遂比心螽斯則繁爾類

人咸知脩其容莫知飾其性之
不飾或愆禮正斧之藻之克念作
聖
出其言善千里應之苟違斯義
同衾以疑

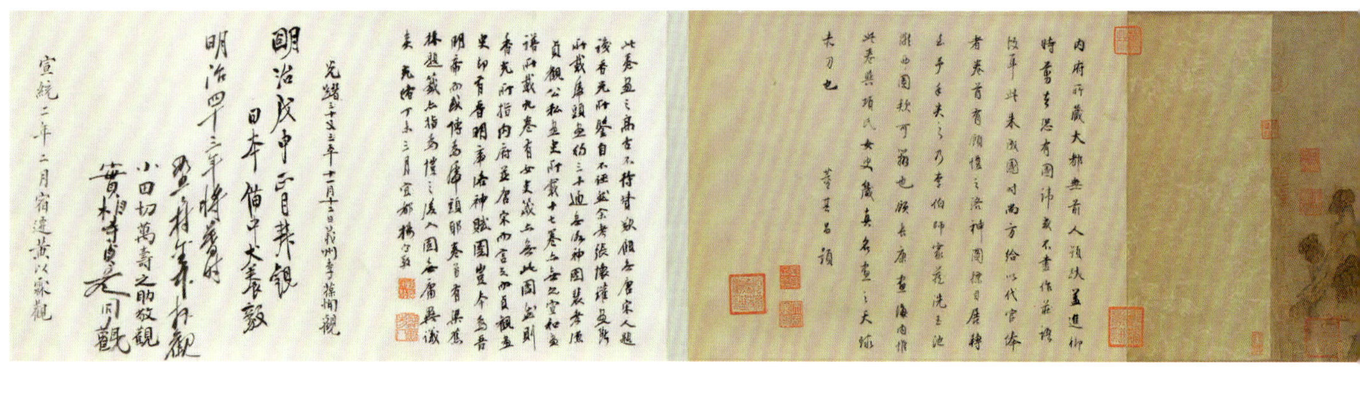

2. 洛神赋图

南宋
（传）顾恺之
绢本设色
手卷
纵24.2、横310.9厘米
弗利尔美术馆

Nymph of Luo River

Southern Song dynasty (1127–1279)
Attributed to Gu Kaizhi
Ink and color on silk
Handscroll
H×W : 24.2×310.9 cm
The Freer Gallery of Art
Gift of Charles Lang Freer

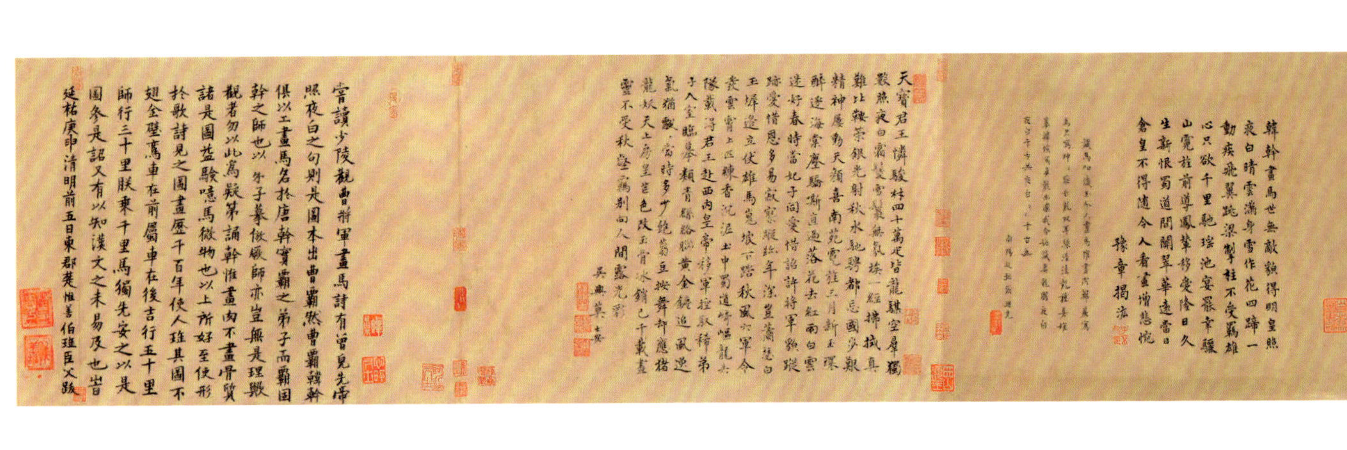

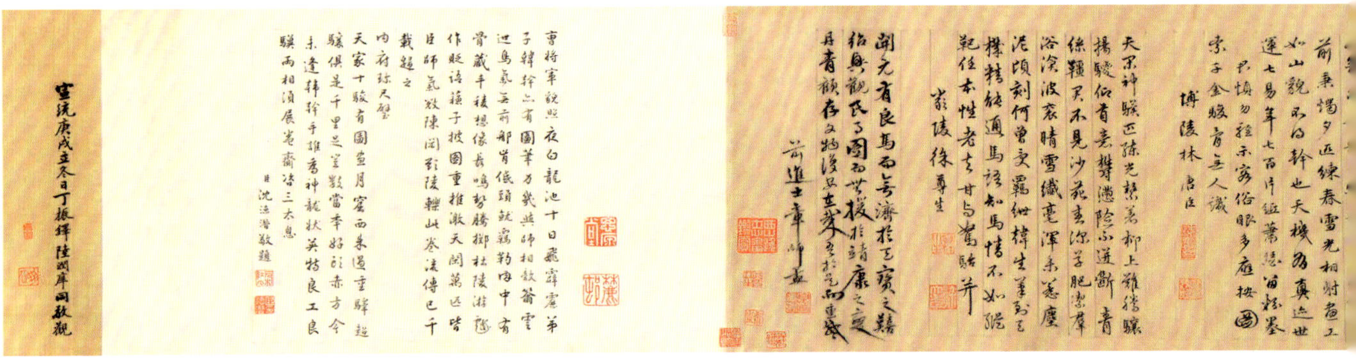

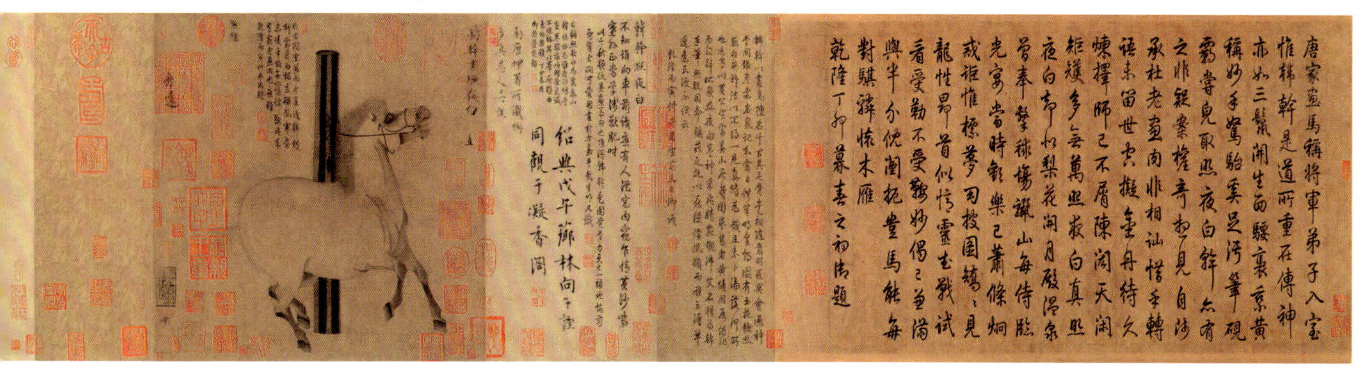

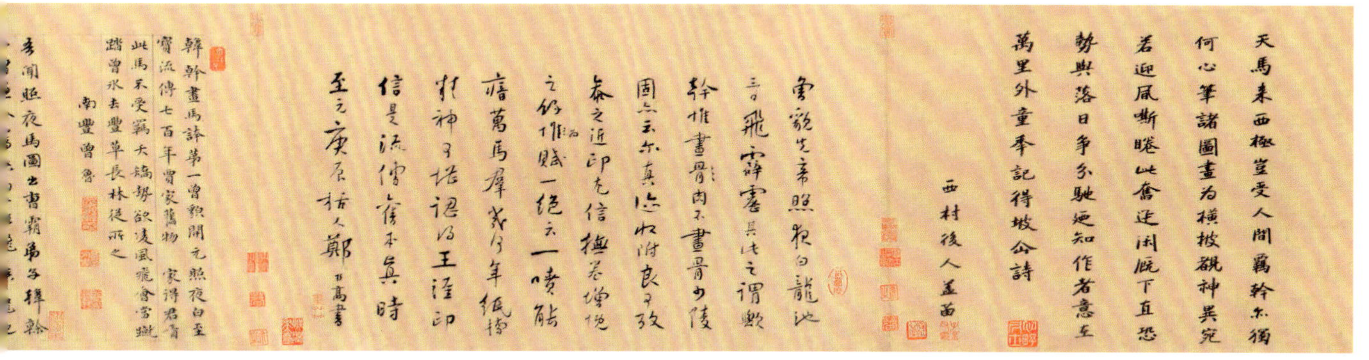

3. 照夜白图

宋或以前
（传）韩幹
纸本水墨
手卷
纵30.8、横34厘米
大都会艺术博物馆

Night-shining White

Song dynasty (960–1279) or earlier
Attributed to Han Gan
Ink on paper
Handscroll
H×W : 30.8×34 cm
The Metropolitan Museum of Art
Purchase, The Dillon Fund Gift, 1977

於古閑空冀而今罕識韓獨
嘶霜月白特立朔風寒宵
志凌金絡無心戀錦韉丹青
曾霸老畫肉也應難
乾隆丙寅仲冬御題

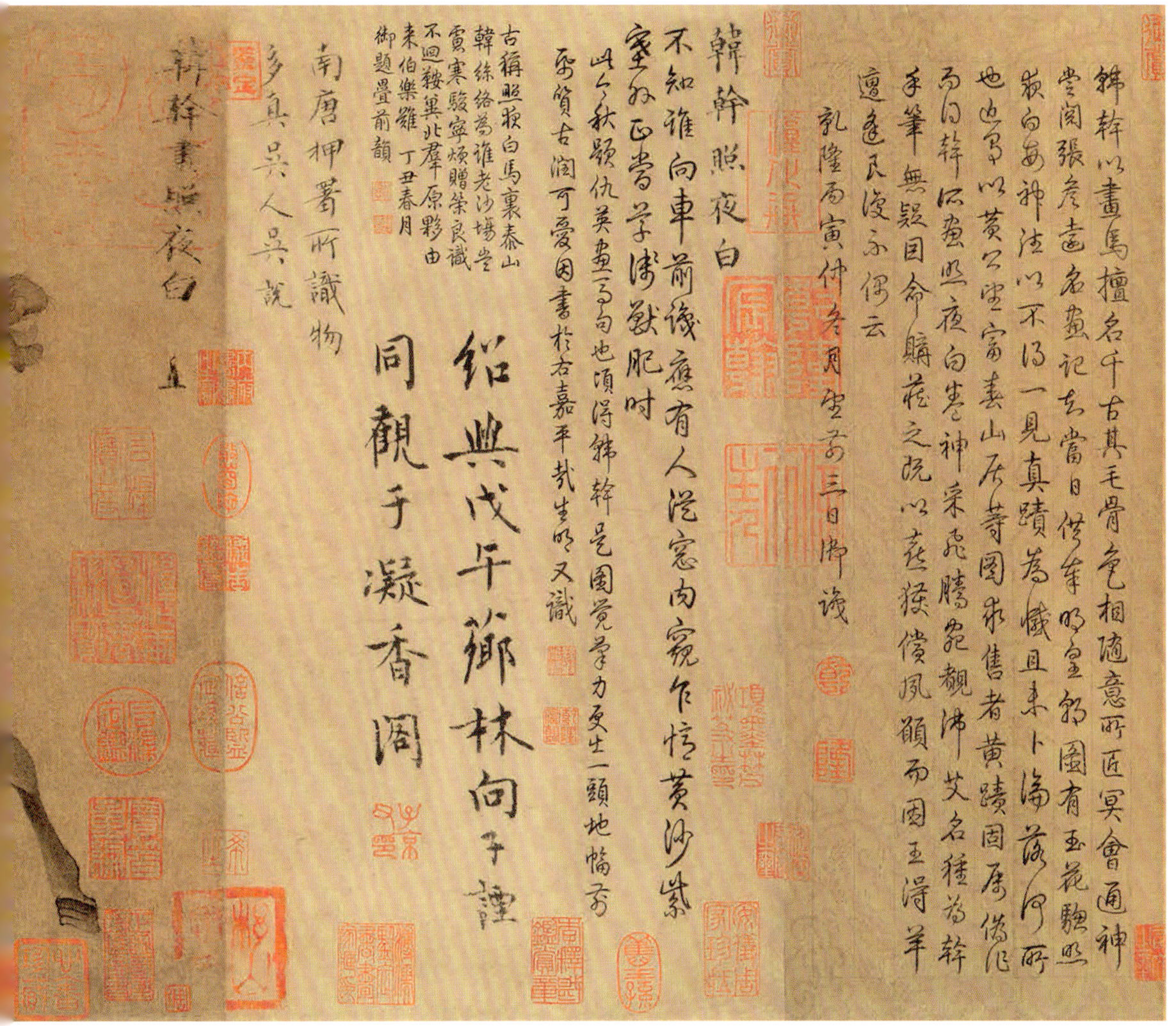
韓幹照夜白
南唐押署所識物
多真吴人吴説
紹興戊午鄰林向子諲同觀于凝香閣

余觀晴齋所藏韓幹圉人呈馬骨肉圓轉精神力健真若出九方皋相法也世可寶之
清容居士袁桷

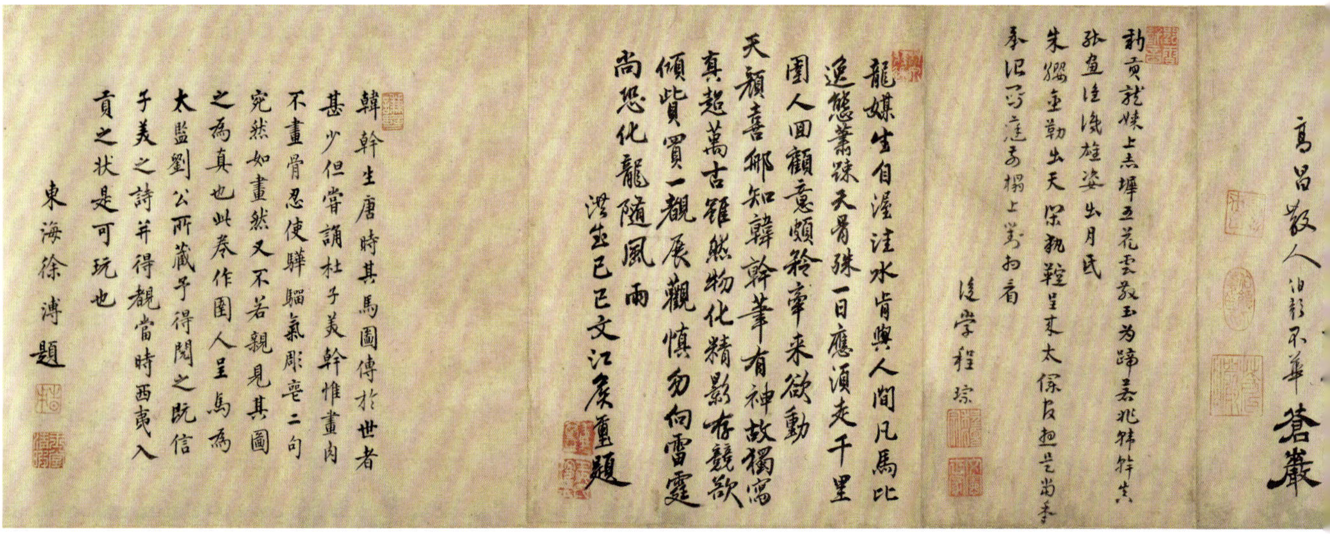
龍媒生自渥洼水肯與人間凡馬比逸態蕭疏天骨殊一日應須走千里圉人回顧意頗矜牽來欲動天顏喜卿知韓幹筆有神故獨寫真超萬古雖然物化精影存競欲傾貲買一觀展觀慎勿向雷霆尚恐化龍隨風雨
韓幹生唐時其馬圖傳於世者甚少但嘗誦杜子美幹惟畫肉不畫骨忍使驊騮氣彫喪二句究然如畫然又不若親見其圖之爲真也此卷作圉人呈馬爲太監劉公所藏予得閱之既信子美之詩并得覩當時西夷入貢之狀是可玩也
東海徐溥題

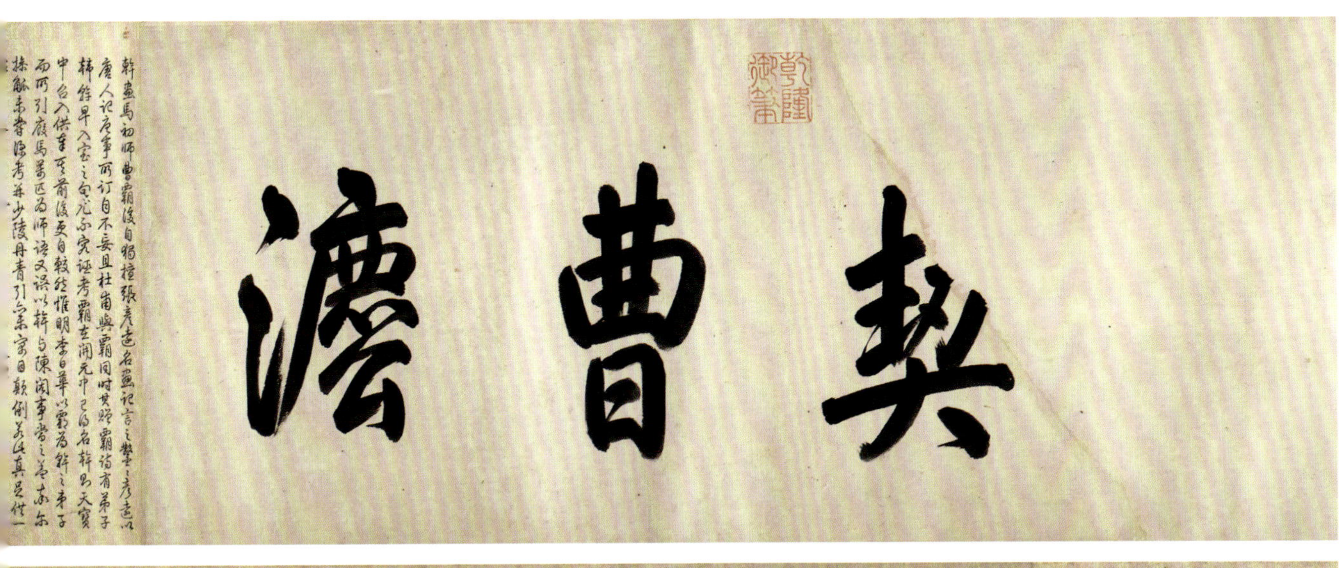

4. 圉人呈马图

宋
（传）韩幹
绢本设色
手卷
纵30.5、横51.4厘米
大都会艺术博物馆

Horse and Groom

Song dynasty (960–1279)
Attributed to Han Gan
Ink and color on silk
Handscroll
H×W : 30.5×51.4 cm
The Metropolitan Museum of Art
From the Collection of A. W. Bahr, Purchase, Fletcher Fund, 1947

韓幹圉人呈馬

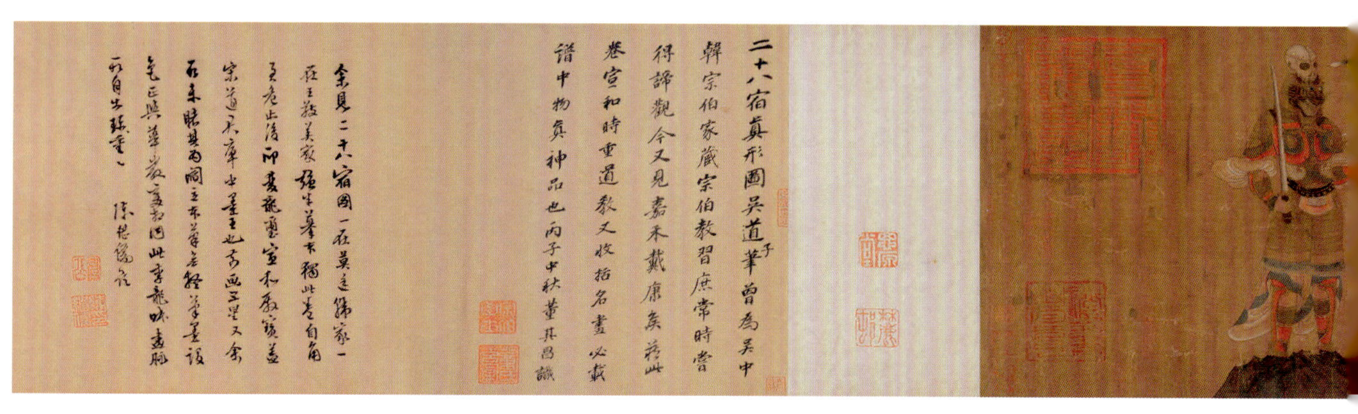

5. 五星二十八宿神形图

北宋
（传）张僧繇
绢本设色
手卷
纵27.5、横489.7厘米
大阪市立美术馆

Five Planets and Twenty-eight Constellations

Northern Song dynasty (960–1127)
Attributed to Zhang Sengyao
Ink and color on silk
Handscroll
H×W : 27.5×489.7 cm
The Osaka City Museum of Fine Arts

6. 送子天王图

北宋
（传）吴道子
纸本水墨
手卷
纵35.7、横338厘米
大阪市立美术馆

Legendary Story of Siddhartha's Birth

Northern Song dynasty (960–1127)
Attributed to Wu Daozi
Ink on paper
Handscroll
H×W : 35.7×338 cm
The Osaka City Museum of Fine Arts

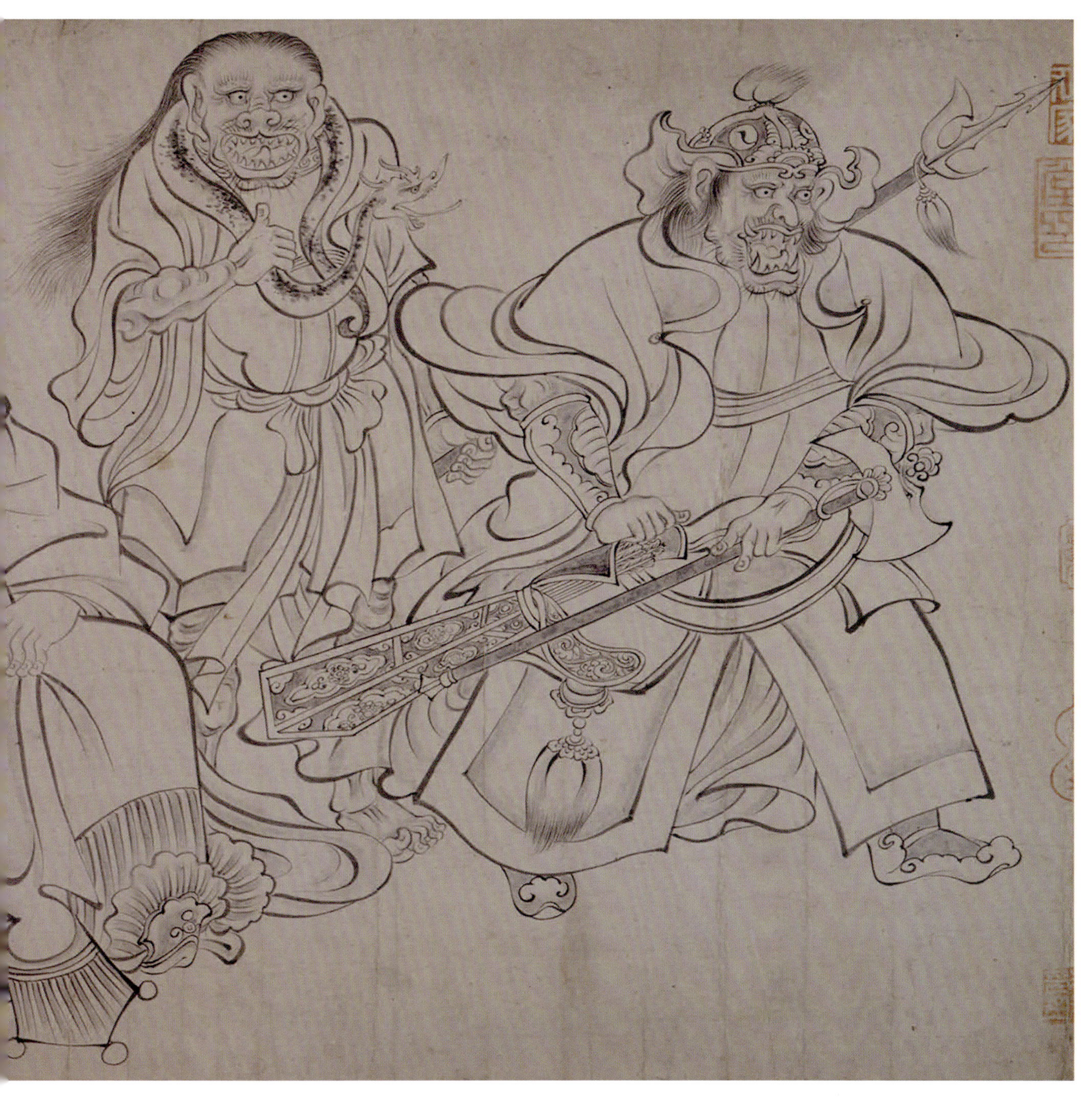

7. 伏生授经图

北宋
（传）王维
绢本设色
手卷
纵25.4、横44.7厘米
大阪市立美术馆

Fu Sheng Expounding Classic

Northern Song dynasty (960–1127)
Attributed to Wang Wei
Ink and color on silk
Handscroll
H×W : 25.4×44.7 cm
The Osaka City Museum of Fine Arts

8. 明皇避暑宫图

Summer Palace of Emperor Ming Huang

北宋
（传）郭忠恕
绢本水墨
立轴
纵161.5、横105.5厘米
大阪市立美术馆

Northern Song dynasty (960–1127)
Attributed to Guo Zhongshu
Ink on silk
Hanging scroll
H×W : 161.5×105.5 cm
The Osaka City Museum of Fine Arts

八十一男子寫神而粗具樂器盆
盂扇椅席鸚鵡犬蝶不與文矩
句容人為江南翰林待詔作士女體
近周昉而加纖麗嘗為後主畫南
莊圖譯一時絶筆它日上之朝廷詔
藉之秘閣宮中圖亦是真蹟藏
前太府卿米載家載摹以見餽
婦人高髻自唐以來如此此卷豐
肌長襦晨周昉法也予至嶠南
於鵠溪陳高祖之裔見其世藏
諸帝像左右宮人梳髻與此略同
而丫髻乃作兩大鬟垂肩項間
雖醜而有真態李氏自謂南唐
故衣冠多用唐制於風流宜承
六朝之餘畫家者亦稱古畫當
先問衣冠車服蓋謂是也紹興
庚申五月乙酉潛亟居士題

9. 宫中图

北宋
（传）周文矩
绢本设色
手卷
纵28.5、横168.6厘米
克利夫兰美术馆

In Palace

Northern Song dynasty (960–1127)
Attributed to Zhou Wenju
Ink and color on silk
Handscroll
H×W : 28.5×168.6 cm
The Cleveland Museum of Art
John L. Severance Fund 1976.1

10. 宫中图

北宋
（传）周文矩
绢本设色
手卷
纵26、横146.7厘米
大都会艺术博物馆

In Palace

Northern Song dynasty (960–1127)
Attributed to Zhou Wenju
Ink and color on silk
Handscroll
H×W : 26×146.7 cm
The Metropolitan Museum of Art
Purchase, Douglas Dillon Gift, 1978

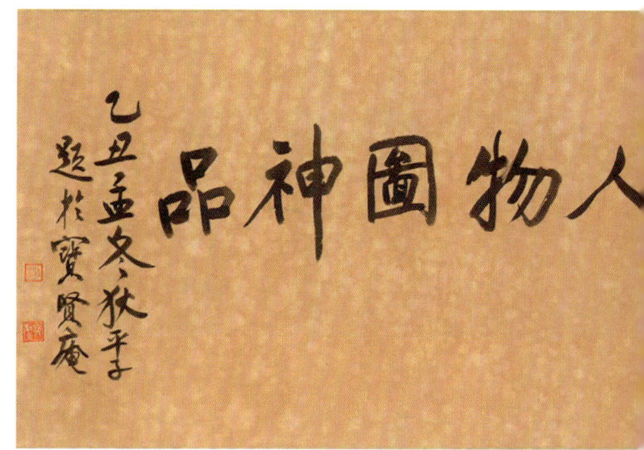

人物圖神品
乙丑孟冬狄平子題於寶賢庵

唐張喬有題上元許棠所任王昌齡廳絕句云琉璃堂裏當時客久絕吟聲繼後塵百四十年庭樹老如今重得見詩人昌齡江寧人江寧後改上元喬咸通間進士略計去昌齡之時近遠亦與詩合所謂瑠璃堂者在金陵無疑故應入江南畫中特未知後咸通又數十年文矩著筆政復為誰耳抑老松偃蹇猶存王許故物耶山陰王易簡

11. 琉璃堂人物图

北宋

（传）周文矩

绢本设色

手卷

纵31.4、横128.4厘米

大都会艺术博物馆

Scholars of Liuli Hall

Northern Song dynasty (960–1127)

Attributed to Zhou Wenju

Ink and color on silk

Handscroll

H×W : 31.4×128.4 cm

The Metropolitan Museum of Art

Gift of Mrs. Sheila Riddell, in memory of Sir Percival David, 1977

周文矩瑠璃堂人物圖
神品工妙也

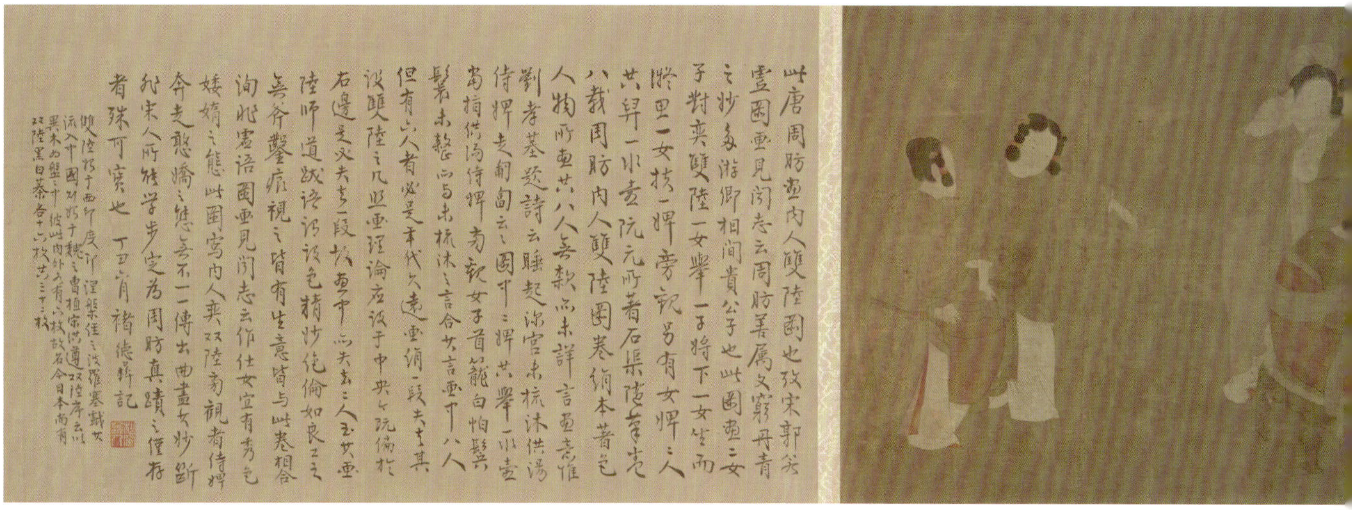
此唐周昉畫內人雙陸圖也攷宋郭若
虛圖畫見聞志云周昉善屬文窮丹青
之妙多游卿相間貴公子也此圖畫二女
子對弈雙陸一女舉一子將下一女坐而
睇思一女捧一盤旁觀另有女婢二人
共舁一水壺阮元所著石渠隨筆亦
載周昉內人雙陸圖卷絹本著色
人物所畫共八人無款亦未詳言畫意惟
劉孝基題詩云睡起深宮未梳沐供湯
侍婢走匆匆云云圖中二婢共舉一水壺
當指供湯侍婢旁觀女子首籠白帕鬟
髻未整亦為未梳沐之言合其言畫中八人
但有六人者必是年代久遠畫絹一段失去其
設雙陸之几與畫理論應設于中央今既偏於
右邊是必失去一段於畫中亦失去二人至其畫
陸師道跋語謂設色精妙絕倫如良工之
無斧鑿痕視之皆有生意皆與此卷相合
詢非虛語圖畫見聞志云作仕女宜有秀色
婑媠之態此圖寫內人弈又雙陸旁觀者侍婢
奔走憨嬌之態無不一一傳出曲盡女妙斷
非宋人所能學步定為周昉真蹟之僅存
者殊可寶也 丁丑六月褚德彝記
雙陸始于西印度
流入中國始于魏之曹植宋洪遵雙陸序云以
異木為盤盤中彼此內外各有六梁故名今日本尚有
雙陸黑白棊各十六枚共三十二枚

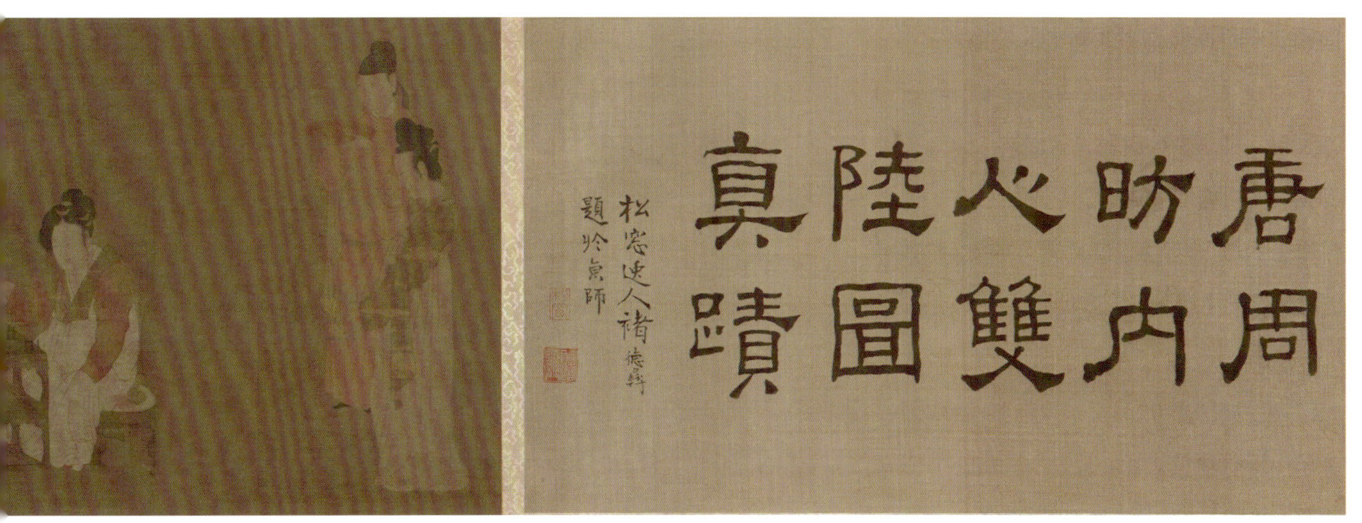

12. 内人双陆图

南宋
（传）周昉
绢本设色
手卷
纵30.5、横69.1厘米
弗利尔美术馆

Palace Ladies Playing Back Gammon

Southern Song dynasty (1127–1279)
Attributed to Zhou Fang
Ink and color on silk
Handscroll
H×W : 30.5×69.1 cm
The Freer Gallery of Art
Purchase–Charles Lang Freer Endowment

13. 二祖调心图

南宋
（传）石恪
纸本水墨
册页
每开：纵35.3、横64.4厘米
东京国立博物馆

Two Patriarchs Harmonizing Their Minds

Southern Song dynasty (1127–1279)
Attributed to Shi Ke
Ink on paper
Album leaf
H×W(each leaf) : 35.3×64.4 cm
The Tokyo National Museum
ColBase(https://colbase.nich.go.jp/collection_items/tnm/TA-162?locale=ja)

14. 竹虫图

Insects and Bamboos

北宋
（传）赵昌
绢本设色
立轴
纵100、横54.5厘米
东京国立博物馆

Northern Song dynasty (960–1127)
Attributed to Zhao Chang
Ink and color on silk
Hanging scroll
H×W : 100×54.5 cm
The Tokyo National Museum
ColBase(https://colbase.nich.go.jp/collection_items/tnm/TA-342?locale=ja)

15. 溪岸图

北宋
（传）董元
绢本设色
立轴
纵220.3、横109.2厘米
大都会艺术博物馆

Riverbank

Northern Song dynasty (960–1127)
Attributed to Dong Yuan
Ink and color on silk
Hanging scroll
H×W : 220.3×109.2 cm
The Metropolitan Museum of Art
Ex coll.: C. C. Wang Family, Gift of Oscar L. Tang Family, in memory of Douglas Dillon, 2016

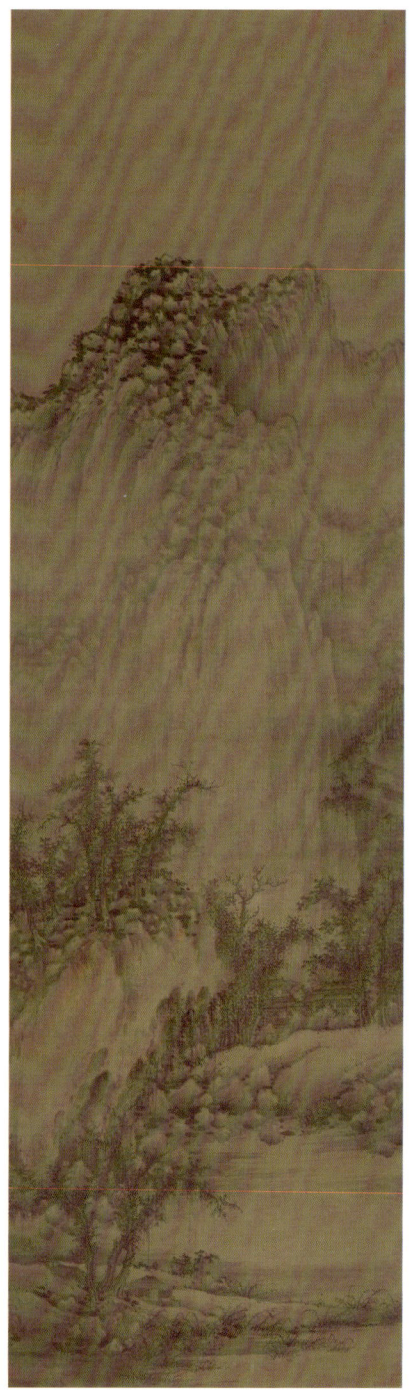

16. 溪山兰若图

北宋
巨然
绢本水墨
立轴
纵184.5、横56.1厘米
克利夫兰美术馆

Buddhist Retreat by Stream and Mountains

Northern Song dynasty (960–1127)
Juran
Ink on silk
Hanging scroll
H×W : 184.5×56.1 cm
The Cleveland Museum of Art
Gift of Katharine Holden Thayer 1959.348

17. 寒林策驴图

北宋
（传）李成
绢本设色
立轴
纵161.9、横100.3厘米
大都会艺术博物馆

Travelers in Wintry Forest

Northern Song dynasty (960–1127)
Attributed to Li Cheng
Ink and color on silk
Hanging scroll
H×W : 161.9×100.3 cm
The Metropolitan Museum of Art
Purchase, Fletcher Fund and Bequest of Dorothy Graham Bennett, 1972

18. 读碑窠石图

北宋
（传）李成、（传）王晓
绢本设色
立轴
纵126.3、横104.9厘米
大阪市立美术馆

Reading Memorial Stele

Northern Song dynasty (960–1127)
Attributed to Li Cheng and Wang Xiao
Ink and color on silk
Hanging scroll
H×W : 126.3×104.9 cm
The Osaka City Museum of Fine Arts

19. 江山楼观图

北宋
（传）燕文贵
纸本设色
手卷
纵32、横161厘米
大阪市立美术馆

Landscape with Pavilions

Northern Song dynasty (960–1127)
Attributed to Yan Wengui
Ink and color on paper
Handscroll
H×W : 32×161 cm
The Osaka City Museum of Fine Arts

20. 江村图

北宋
（传）燕文贵
绢本设色
册页
纵24.1、横25.4厘米
大都会艺术博物馆

River Hamlet

Northern Song dynasty (960–1127)
Attributed to Yan Wengui
Ink and color on silk
Album leaf
H×W : 24.1×25.4 cm
The Metropolitan Museum of Art
Bequest of John M. Crawford Jr., 1988

21. 夏山图

北宋
（传）屈鼎
绢本设色
手卷
纵45.4、横115.3厘米
大都会艺术博物馆

Summer Mountains

Northern Song dynasty (960–1127)
Attributed to Qu Ding
Ink and color on silk
Handscroll
H×W : 45.4×115.3 cm
The Metropolitan Museum of Art
Ex coll.: C. C. Wang Family, Gift of The Dillon Fund, 1973

22. 雪山楼阁图

北宋
（传）范宽
绢本设色
立轴
纵182.4、横103厘米
波士顿艺术博物馆

Winter Landscape with Temples

Northern Song dynasty (960–1127)
Attributed to Fan Kuan
Ink and color on silk
Hanging scroll
H×W : 182.4×103 cm
The Museum of Fine Arts, Boston
Chinese and Japanese Special Fund

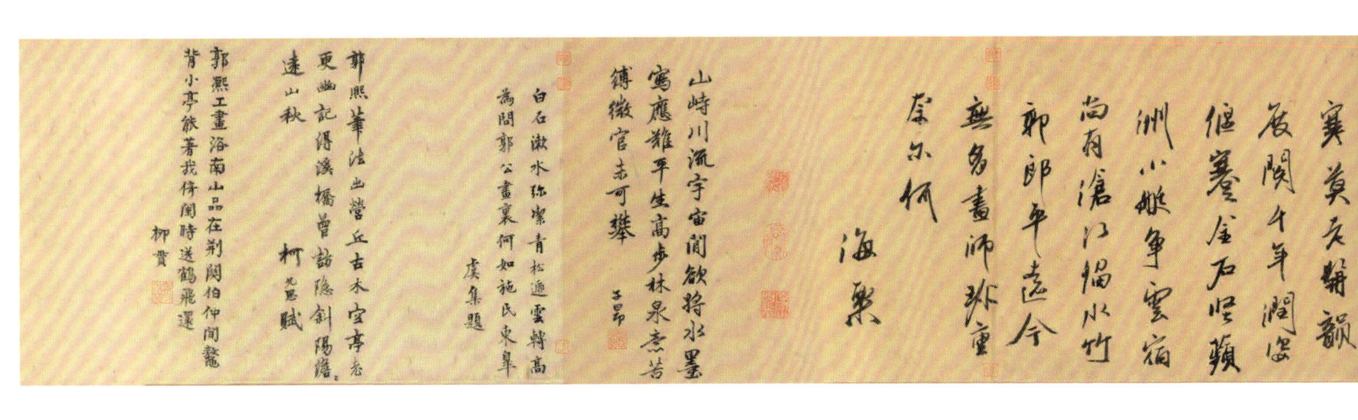

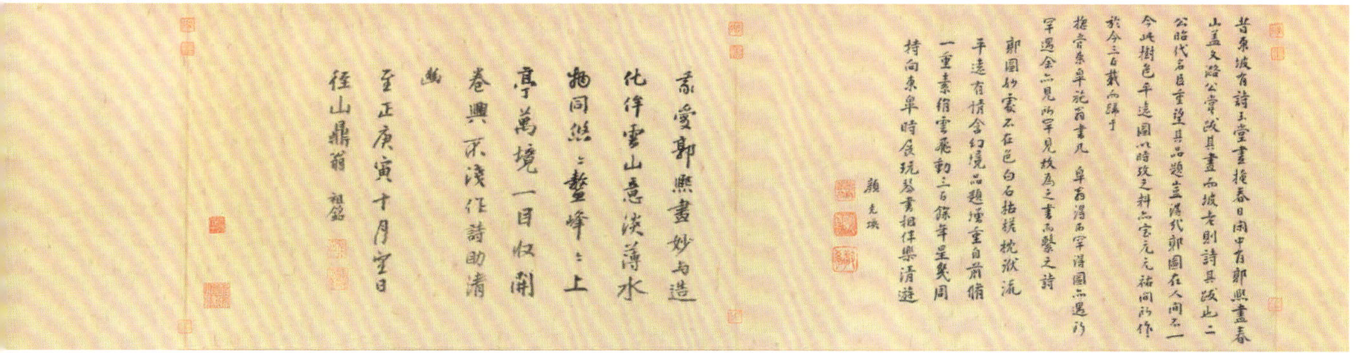

23. 树色平远图

北宋
郭熙
绢本设色
手卷
纵35.6、横104.4厘米
大都会艺术博物馆

Old Trees, Level Distance

Northern Song dynasty (960–1127)
Guo Xi
Ink and color on silk
Handscroll
H×W : 35.6×104.4 cm
The Metropolitan Museum of Art
Gift of John M. Crawford Jr., in honor of Douglas Dillon, 1981

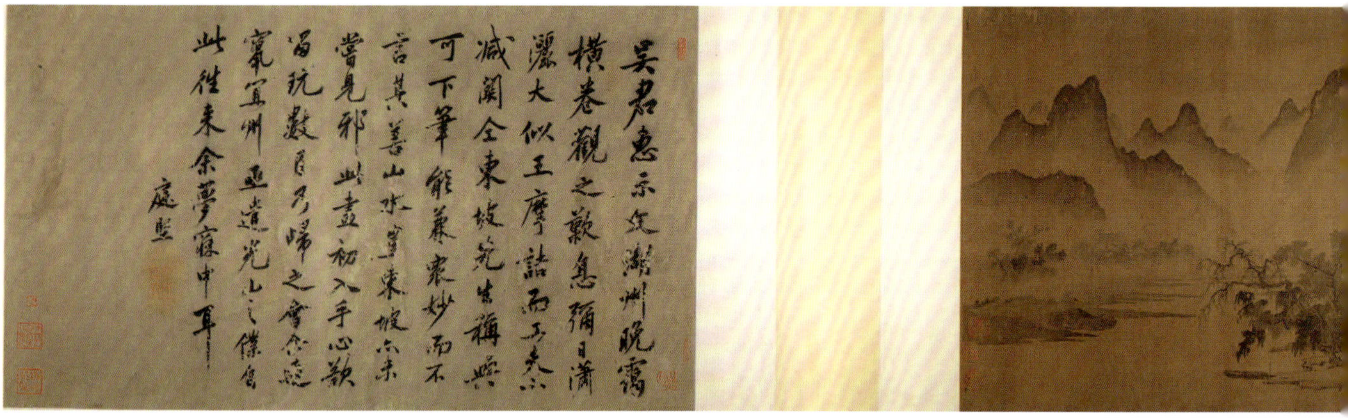

24. 晚霭图

北宋
（传）文同
绢本设色
手卷
纵55.9、横256.5厘米
大都会艺术博物馆

Rosy Sunset

Northern Song dynasty (960–1127)
Attributed to Wen Tong
Ink and color on silk
Handscroll
H×W : 55.9×256.5 cm
The Metropolitan Museum of Art
Rogers Fund, 1919

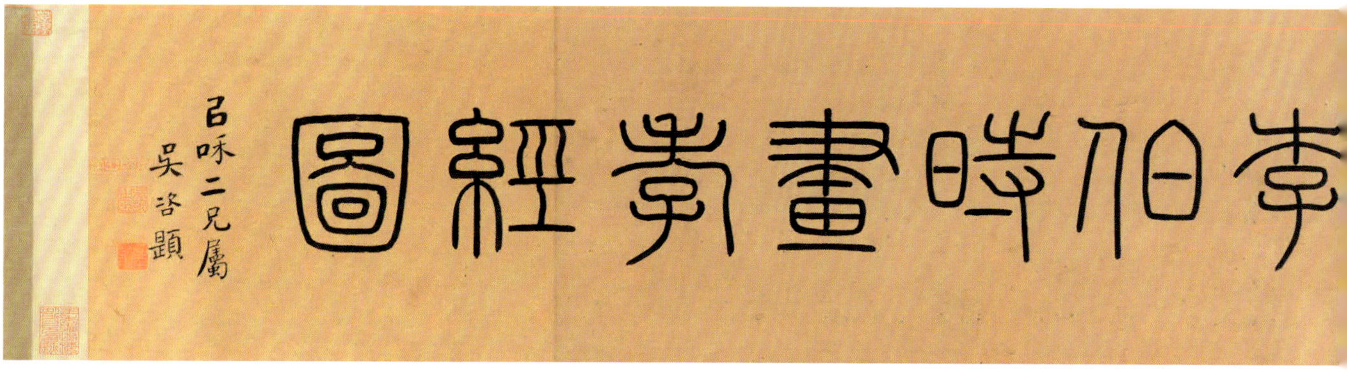
李伯時畫孝經圖
呂咊二兄屬
吳咨題

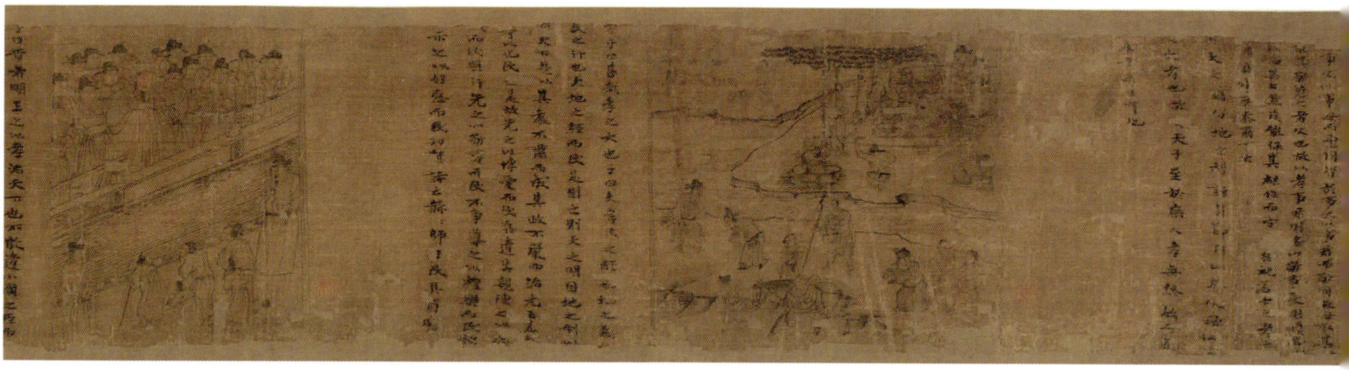

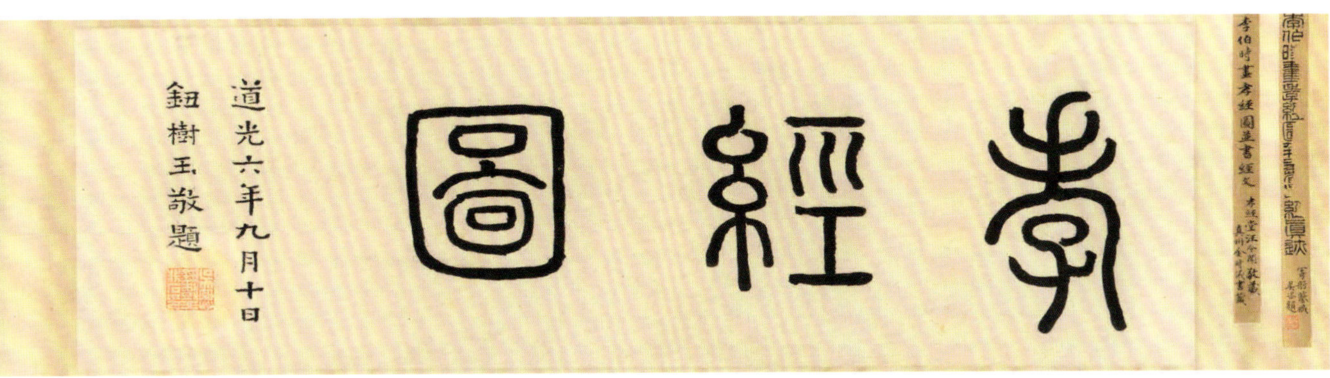

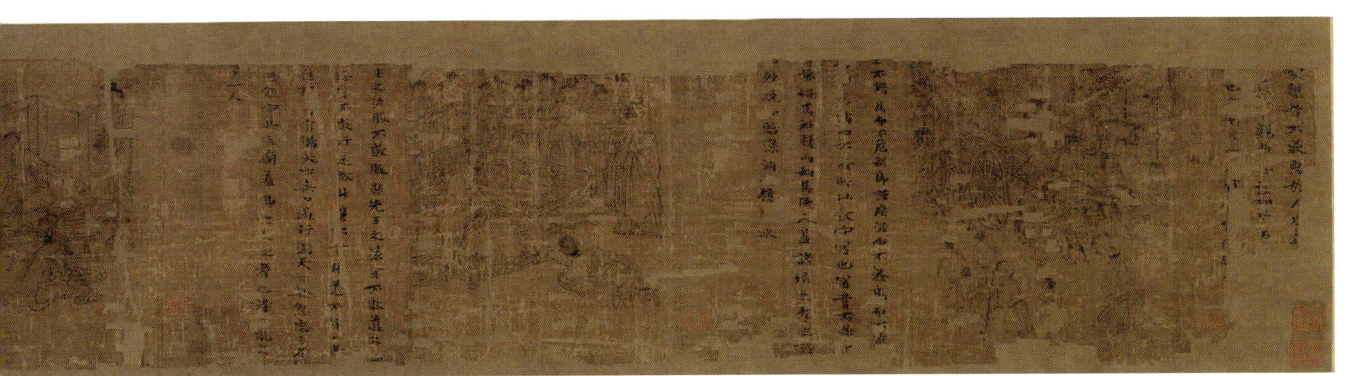

25. 孝经图

北宋

（传）李公麟

绢本设色

手卷

纵21.9、横475.6厘米

大都会艺术博物馆

Classic of Filial Piety

Northern Song dynasty (960–1127)

Attributed to Li Gonglin

Ink and color on silk

Handscroll

H×W : 21.9×475.6 cm

The Metropolitan Museum of Art

Ex coll.: C. C. Wang Family, From the P. Y. and Kinmay W. Tang Family Collection, Gift of Oscar L. Tang Family, 1996

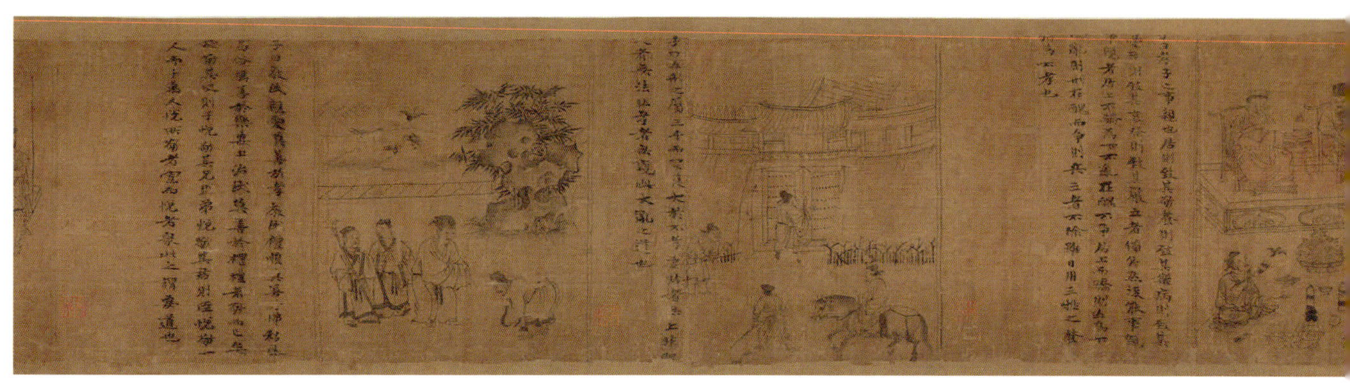

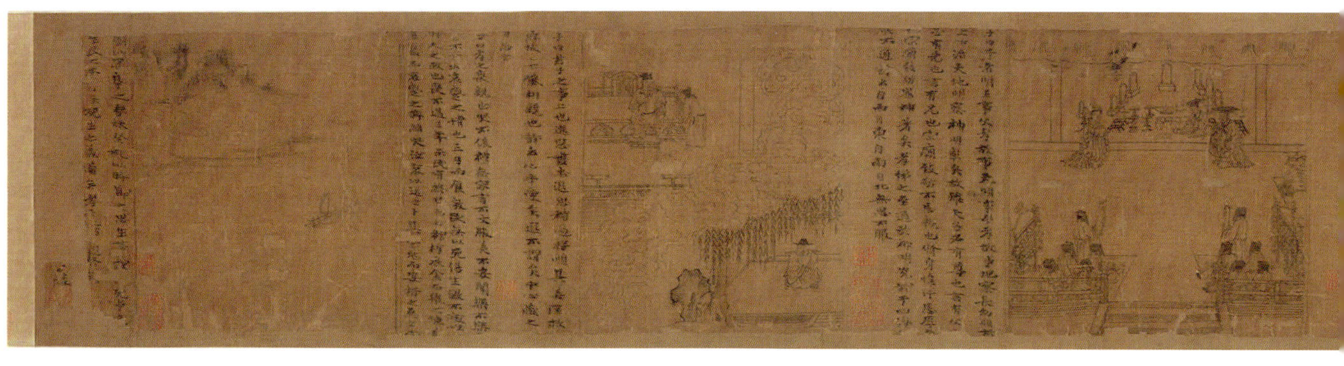

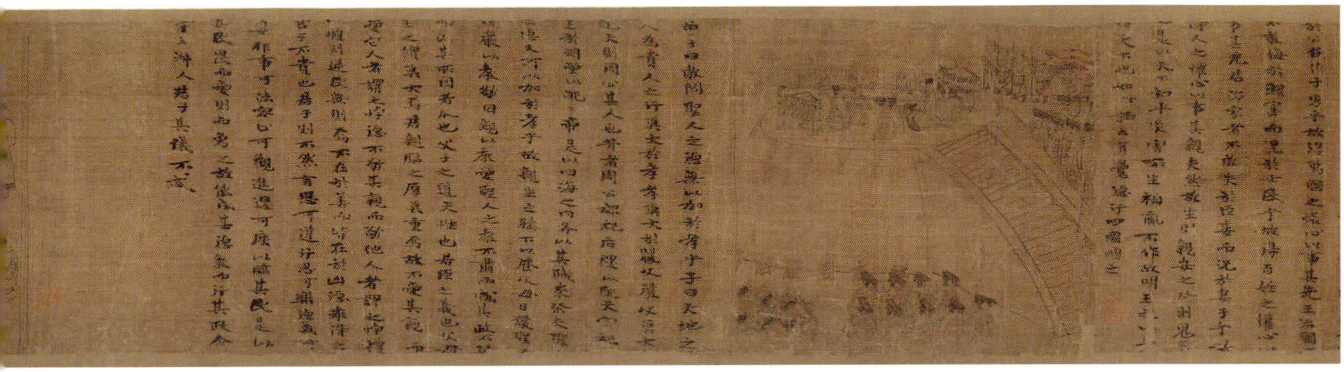

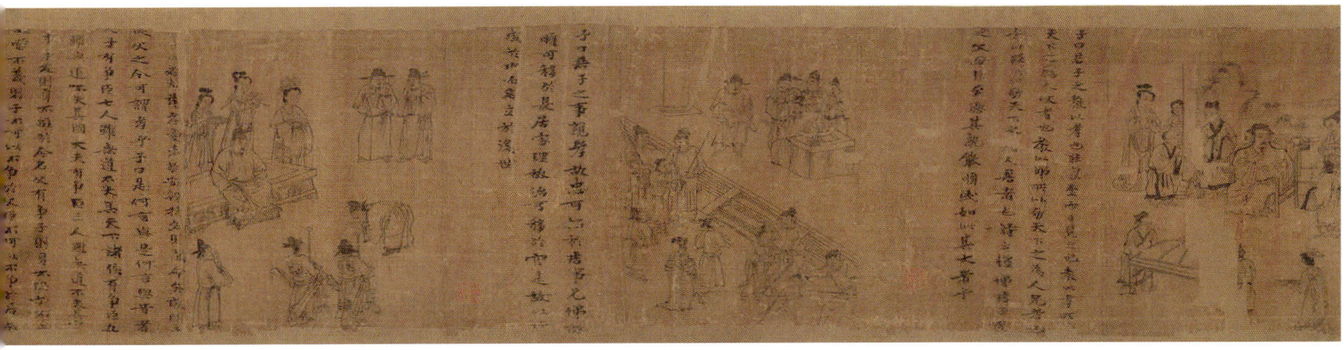

有益於世教者豈獨書美
觀云乎哉如縱如虎萬筆
不忝展卷三玩可以寶諸
篋在上章攝提格之相
月汗漫翁書

卷中般教二字俱不全以避宋廟諱

周密煙雲過眼録載
李伯時畫孝經并書
即此卷也伯時畫孝
經名款此卷獨有以
麟名款者是進御
作乃是可以歆

新都劉太學抑真令之孝
子閱余有此卷以趙文敏
秋林撫琴圖相易太學
又從贈東坡書金剛經石
榻旋海內之誦持者發
敬信心以資冥福先請
余書額經者三大字置
之內舍今以石在西洞庭
一居士家訪之未獲大以昔

迹之妙不減顧陸至第十八章人子之
所不忍者獨寫其歸歸非有道君子
不能爲然非顧陸之所及東坡所跋大
約即此卷也是葉蘊書時劉去耳 竹嬾

陳眉公眠古錄云龍眠書法山谷謂其魚
之鬭鈕遠入書中今觀此孝經小楷樸朴
中神彩煥發覺古隸典刑具在玉露叢之
精華香光所謂直追鍾頭者其希世之珍
千金不易者也

董文敏以己酉三月易此卷於新安劉太學余得此卷
己酉後五月相距已一百八十年矣余亦新安人一奇事
也皆有墨緣存焉耳 己酉秋八月望日竹嬾記

道光六年重陽後一日與商
邱宋端己江寧楊大堉陽城
張葆采集于保澄軒同觀此
卷吳縣鈕樹玉敬記

李伯時孝經圖每章摘經一二語其處幻奇
妙更出聖賢道處二圖之上至其書則前人
謂其力追鍾語語不虛也姚惜抱先生自言
家在龍眠而生平未見伯時之畫今內之數
歲中而得其可寶者三焉其亦可以知足矣
道光七年夏五月上元管同跋

李龍眠畫宋魏晉宣和譜所載此卷乃學鍾元常薦季直表卷宋有公麟名款他卷無是也余摹刻戲鴻堂帖卷若其畫法之妙直追虎頭吾稱二絕

董其昌題于戲鴻堂

龍眠居士李公麟字伯時舒城大族家世業儒父虚一嘗舉賢良方正公麟以熙寧三年登第陸佃薦為中書省刪定官董敦逸辟充御史臺檢法生平五朝歸事籍籍有聲遊戲翰墨之餘留情畫畫心通意適直造玄妙一補龍眠所作佛像追吴道子山水類李思訓人物似韓滉尤好畫馬有所謂五花散駿萬里汗血往往以觀練闕韓餘之徒故坡詩云龍眠胸中有千駟不惟畫肉兼畫骨山谷亦云伯時作馬如孫太古湔滌水石似王摩詰謂其筆力俊逸故也晚年得僧秀鐵面斥之曰不可畫馬恐日後淪其趣於是翻然絕筆乃刻意於佛像或有餘閑時作人物每能出奇五異此人事盡絕使寒於生笋冰池出魚況此石在人間當如優鉢羅花千年一現耶印之願力終當傳千一回觀此卷除之

乙酉三月廿一日

董其昌

桐城方貞觀江都方士庶吴大治同觀

李伯時孝經圖卷書法鍾王畫追顧陸董文敏稱為二絕洵希世之珍也據董跋是卷以乙酉年歸新安劉幼真太學家當是萬曆三十七年至國朝嘉慶己卯歸予家凡二百十矣中間收藏可考者明人為劉太學入本朝則江進璋字令聞歙邑富商嘗為是卷造孝經樓以貯之備極珍重後又歸畢尚書沅之弟畢瀧家己卯歲予睹於繁昌鮑氏獲歸齋中劉太學暨江令聞皆徽郡人畢尚書本籍新安予亦籍隸新安計二百數十年中此卷展轉皆未出吾郡豈非翰墨緣深冥冥者有默相呵護使神物不離斯土耶是卷爲孝經先賢遺蹟有關於名教甚大不僅以筆墨之妙超前絕後為足重也後之人所宜深思永念以期慎守勿失焉矣

洪瑩記

余所見龍眠畫傳者十之八九如此圖孝經品格已高書法亦妙絕可稱天下龍眠畫第一實萬金之寶也

平洲記

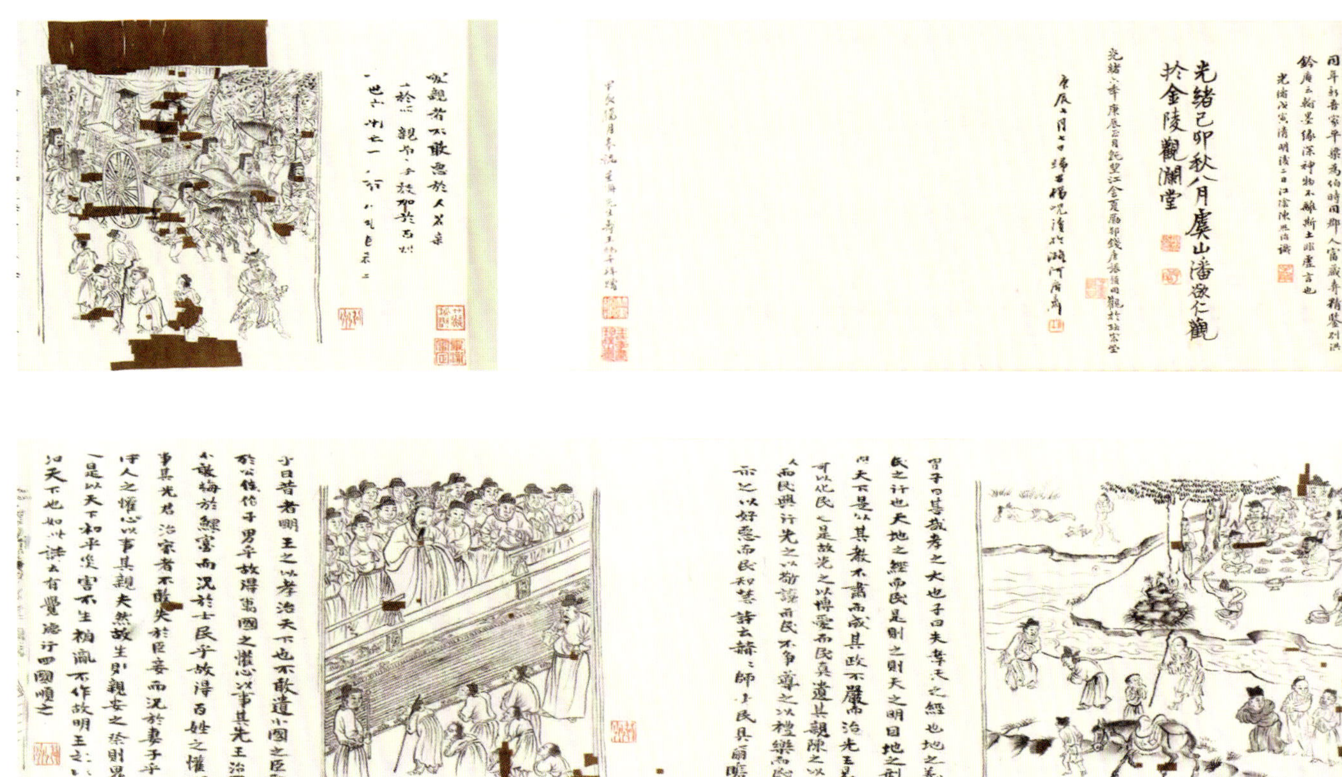

上不驕，高而不危；制節謹度，滿而不溢。高而不危，所以長守貴也；滿而不溢，所以長守富也。富貴不離其身，然後能保其社稷，而和其民人，蓋諸侯之孝也。詩云：戰戰兢兢，如臨深淵，如履薄冰。

非先王之法服不敢服，非先王之法言不敢道，非先王之德行不敢行。是故非法不言，非道不行；口無擇言，身無擇行；言滿天下無口過，行滿天下無怨惡。三者備矣，然後能守其宗廟，蓋卿大夫之孝也。詩云：夙夜匪懈，以事一人。

資於事父以事母而愛同，資於事父以事君而敬同。故母取其愛，而君取其敬，兼之者父也。故以孝事君則忠，以敬事長則順。忠順不失，以事其上，然後能保其祿位，而守其祭祀，蓋士之孝也。詩云：夙興夜寐，無忝爾所生。

用天之道，分地之利，謹身節用，以養父母，此庶人之孝也。故自天子至於庶人，孝無終始，而患不及者，未之有也。

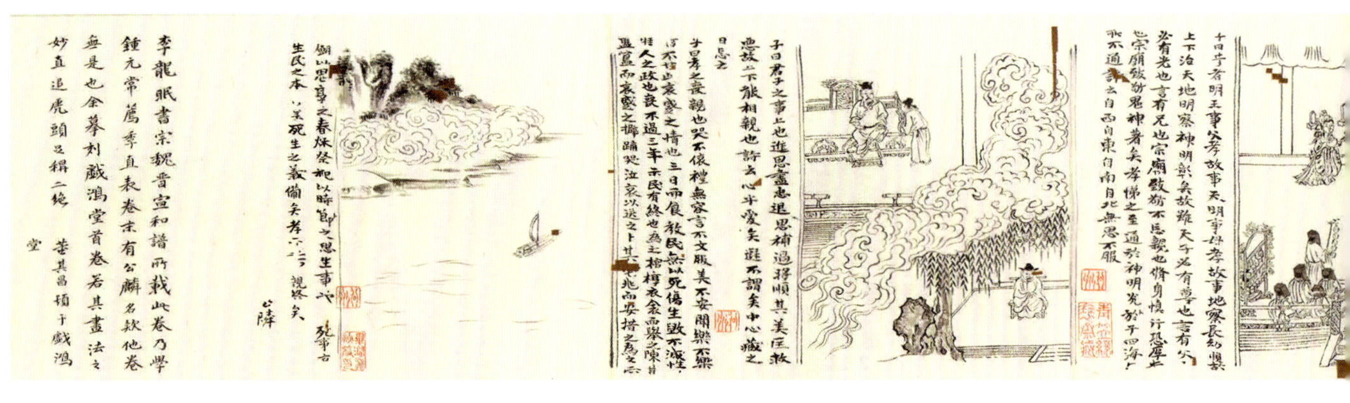
李龍眠書宗魏晉宣和譜所載此卷乃學
鍾元常薦季直表卷末有公麟名款他卷
無是也余摹刻戲鴻堂首卷若其畫法之
妙直追虎頭以稱二絶
董其昌題于戲鴻
堂

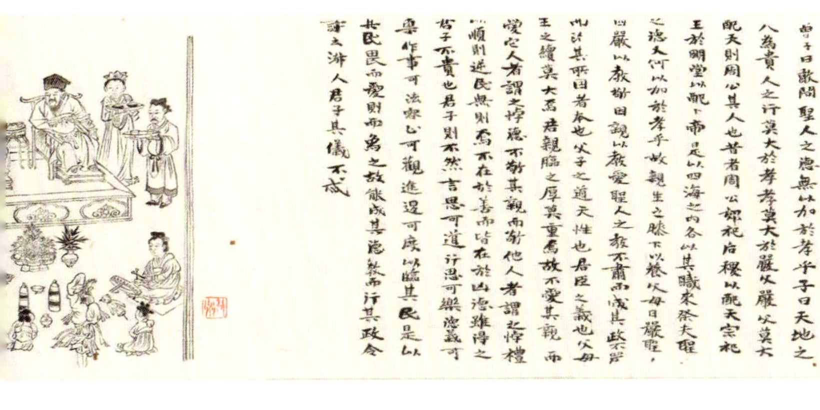

曾子曰：敢問聖人之德，無以加於孝乎？子曰：天地之性，人為貴。人之行，莫大於孝。孝莫大於嚴父，嚴父莫大於配天，則周公其人也。昔者周公郊祀后稷以配天，宗祀文王於明堂以配上帝。是以四海之內，各以其職來祭。夫聖人之德，又何以加於孝乎？故親生之膝下，以養父母日嚴。聖人因嚴以教敬，因親以教愛。聖人之教不肅而成，其政不嚴而治，其所因者本也。父子之道，天性也，君臣之義也。父母生之，續莫大焉。君親臨之，厚莫重焉。故不愛其親而愛他人者，謂之悖德；不敬其親而敬他人者，謂之悖禮。以順則逆，民無則焉。不在於善，而皆在於凶德，雖得之，君子不貴也。君子則不然，言思可道，行思可樂，德義可尊，作事可法，容止可觀，進退可度，以臨其民。是以其民畏而愛之，則而象之。故能成其德教，而行其政令。詩云：淑人君子，其儀不忒。

子曰：君子之教以孝也，非家至而日見之也。教以孝，所以敬天下之為人父者也；教以悌，所以敬天下之為人兄者也；教以臣，所以敬天下之為人君者也。詩云：愷悌君子，民之父母。非至德，其孰能順民如此其大者乎？

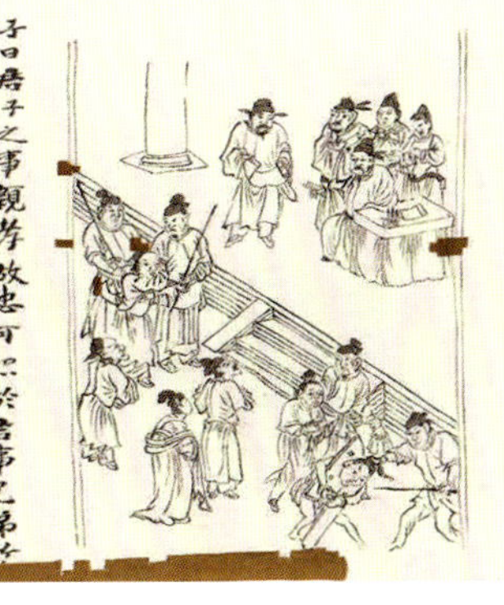

子曰：君子之事親孝，故忠可移於君；事兄悌，故順可移於長；居家理，故治可移於官。是故行成於內，而名立於後世矣。

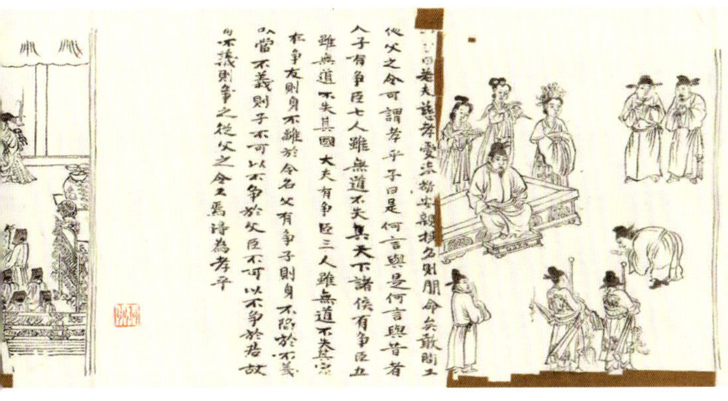

曾子曰：若夫慈愛恭敬，安親揚名，則聞命矣。敢問子從父之令，可謂孝乎？子曰：是何言與！是何言與！昔者天子有爭臣七人，雖無道，不失其天下；諸侯有爭臣五人，雖無道，不失其國；大夫有爭臣三人，雖無道，不失其家；士有爭友，則身不離於令名；父有爭子，則身不陷於不義。故當不義，則子不可以不爭於父，臣不可以不爭於君。故當不義則爭之。從父之令，又焉得為孝乎？

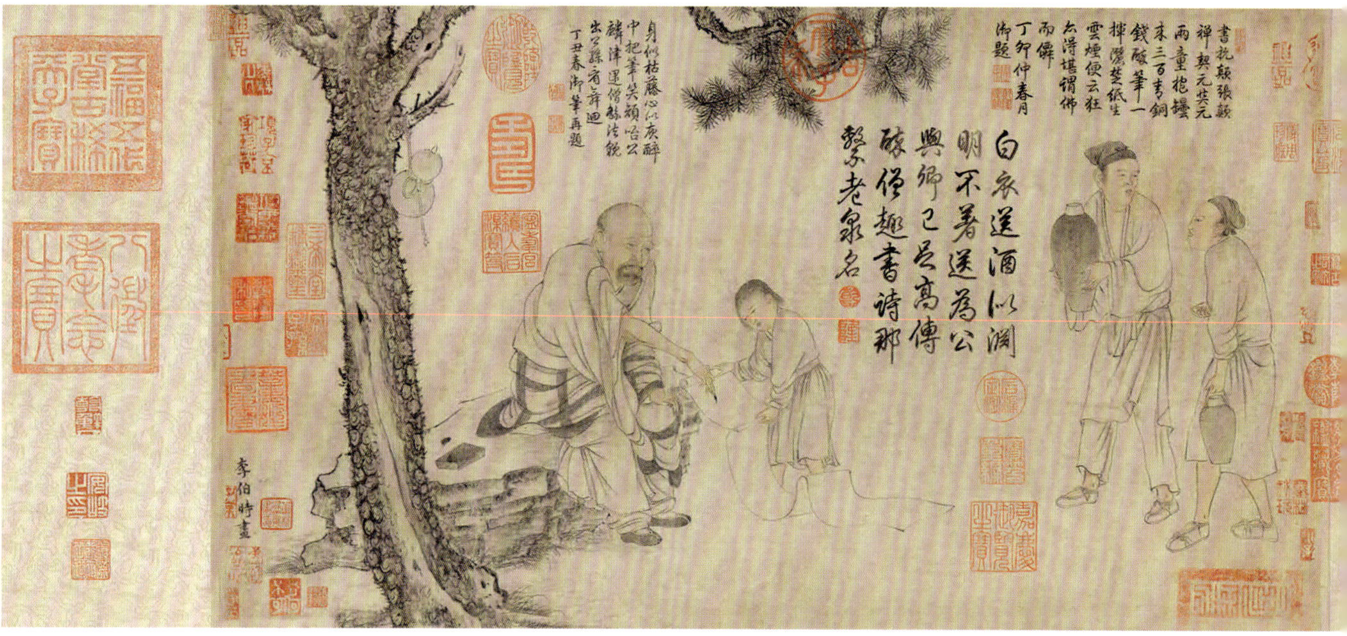
李伯時畫

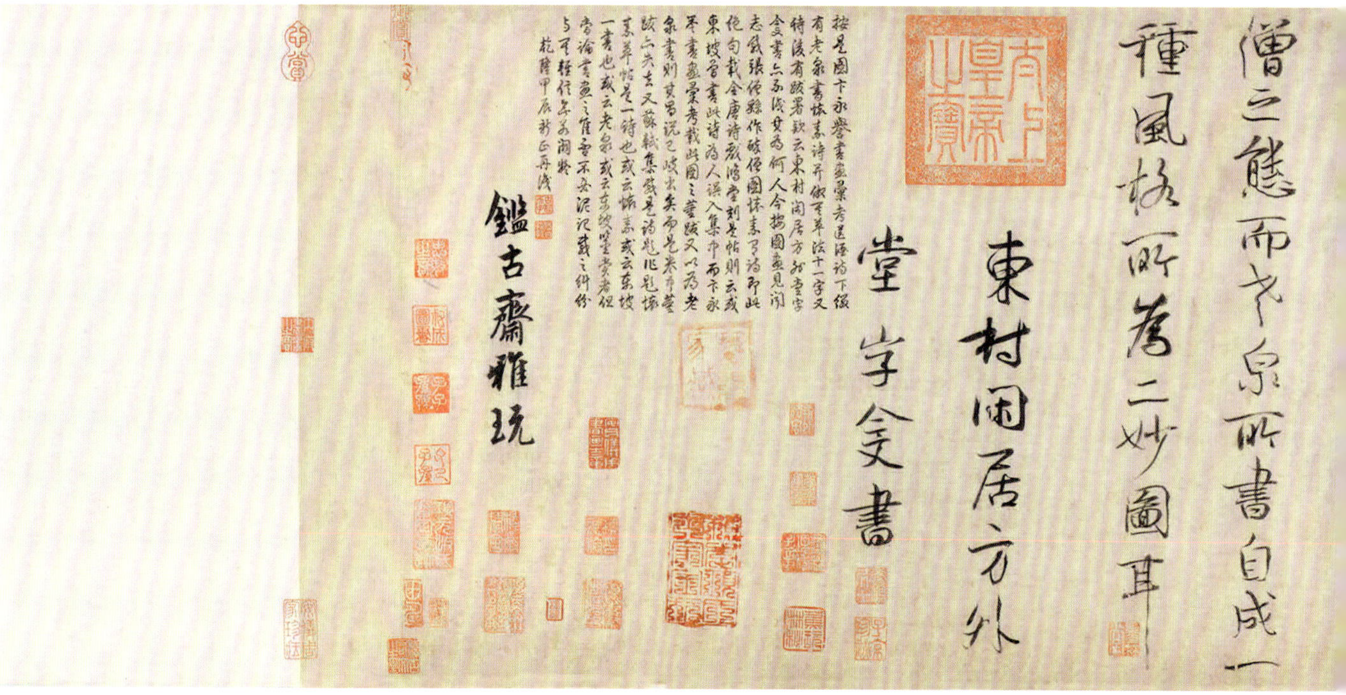
鑑古齋雅玩

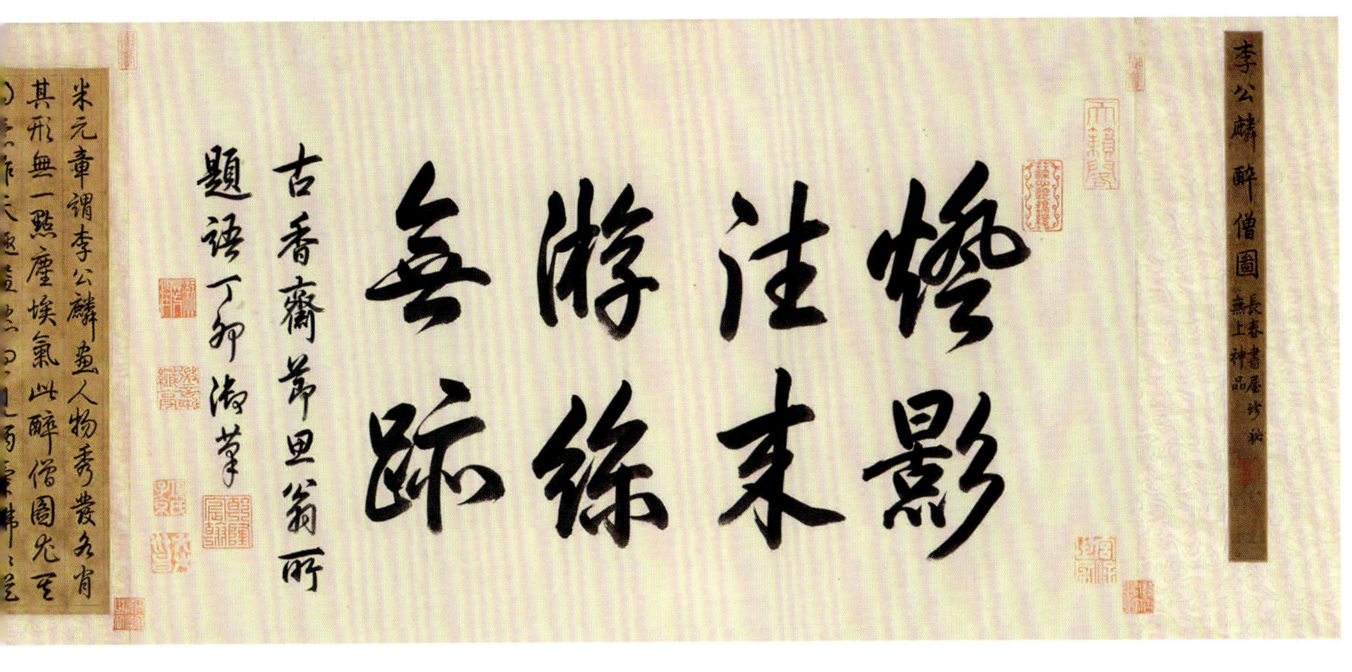

26. 醉僧图

南宋
（传）李公麟
纸本设色
手卷
纵32.5、横60.8厘米
弗利尔美术馆

Drunken Monk

Southern Song dynasty (1127–1279)
Attributed to Li Gonglin
Ink and color on paper
Handscroll
H×W : 32.5×60.8 cm
The Freer Gallery of Art
Gift of Eugene and Agnes E. Meyer

身似枯藤心似灰醉
中把筆笑頻咍公
丁丑春御筆再題
李伯時畫

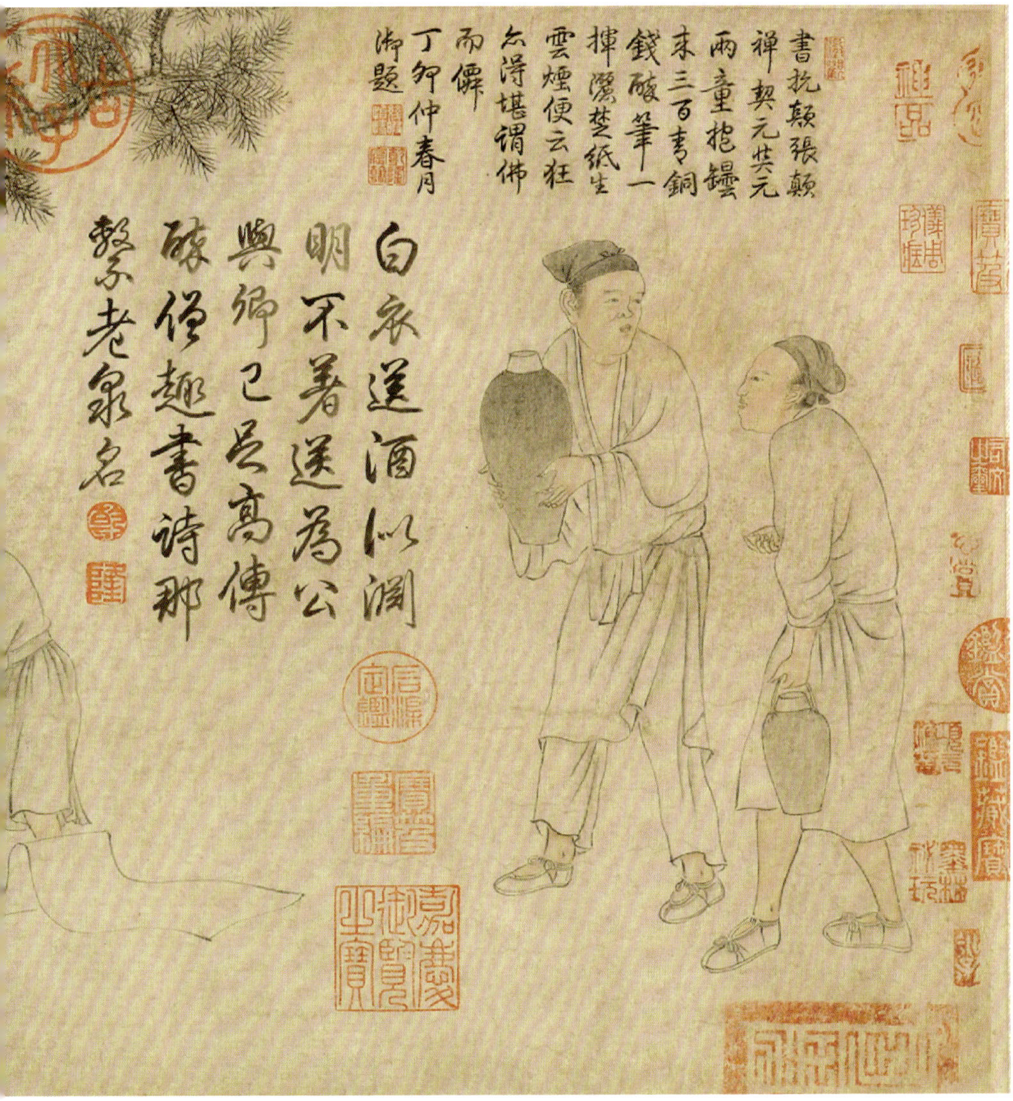
丁卯仲春月
御題

海上顧中舍所藏名卷有四謂顧愷之女史箴李
伯時蜀江圖九歌圖及此瀟湘圖耳女史在檇李
項家九歌在余家瀟湘在陳子有參政家蜀江在
信陽王思延將軍家皆奇珍也 董其昌觀因題

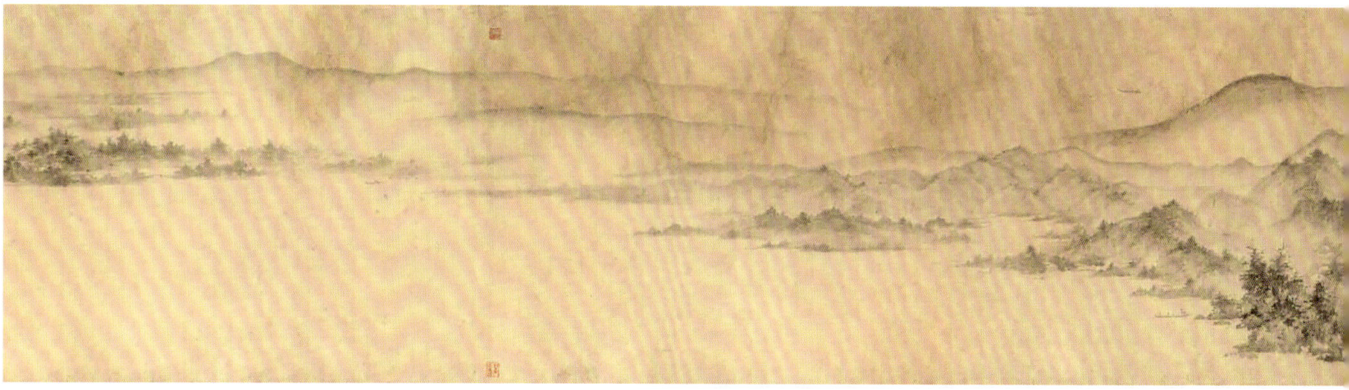

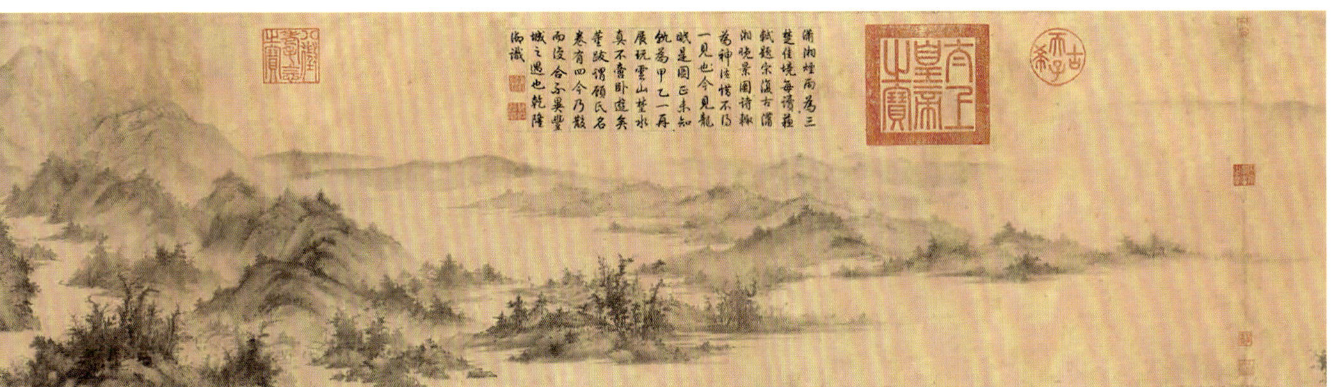

27. 潇湘卧游图

南宋
李氏
纸本水墨
手卷
纵30.3、横400.4厘米
东京国立博物馆

Imaginary Tour Through Xiao Xiang Region

Southern Song dynasty (1127–1279)
Artist Li
Ink on paper
Handscroll
H×W : 30.3×400.4 cm
The Tokyo National Museum
ColBase(https://colbase.nich.go.jp/collection_items/tnm/TA-161?locale=ja)

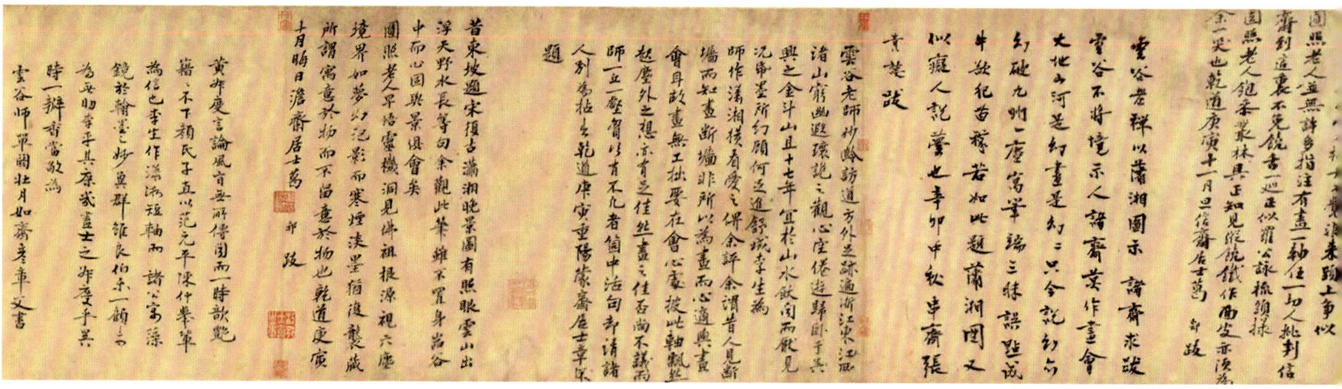

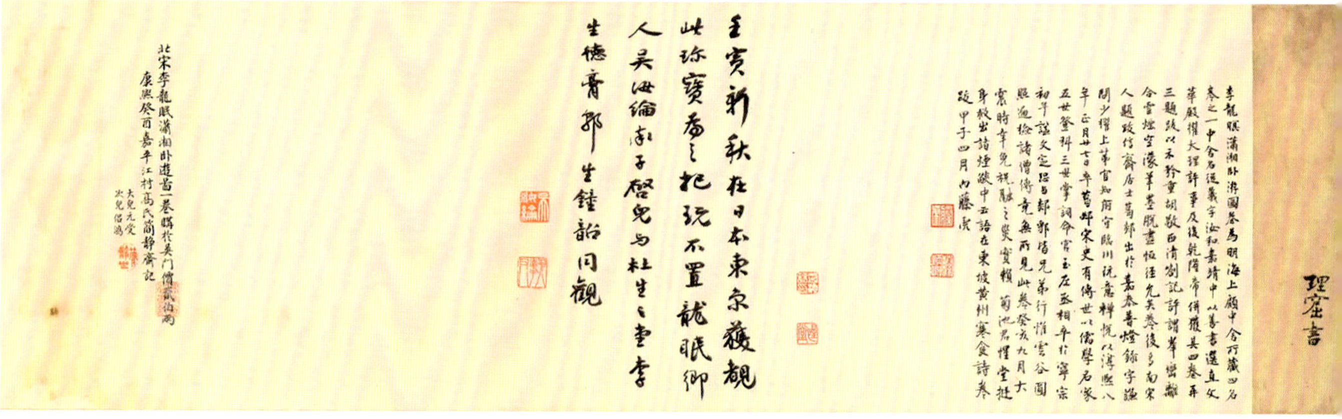

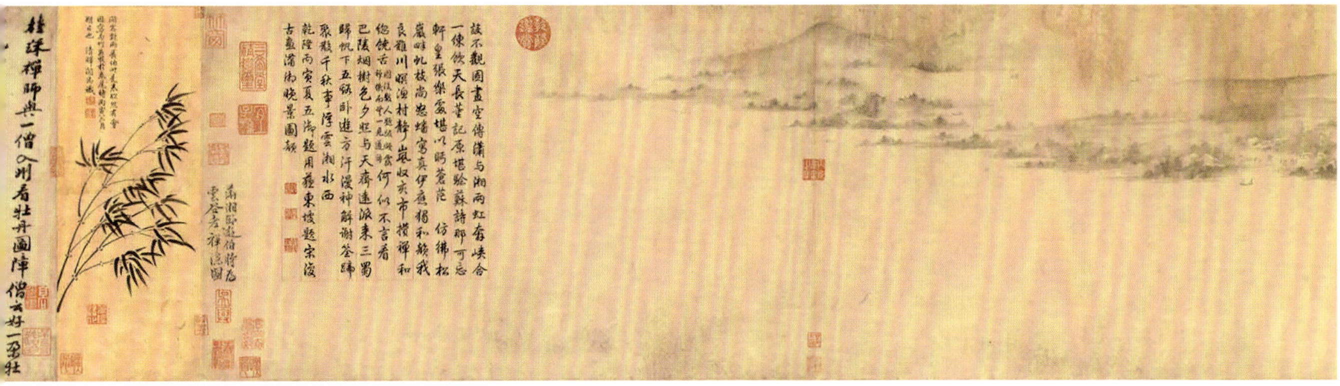

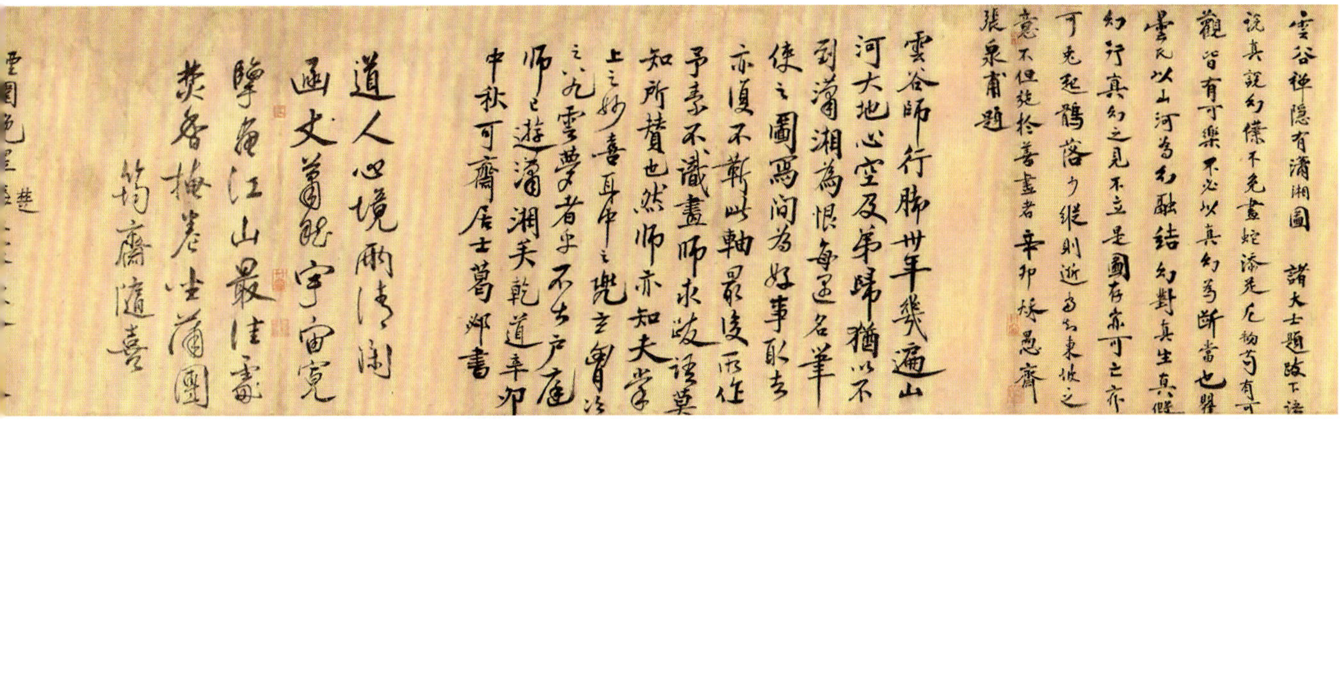

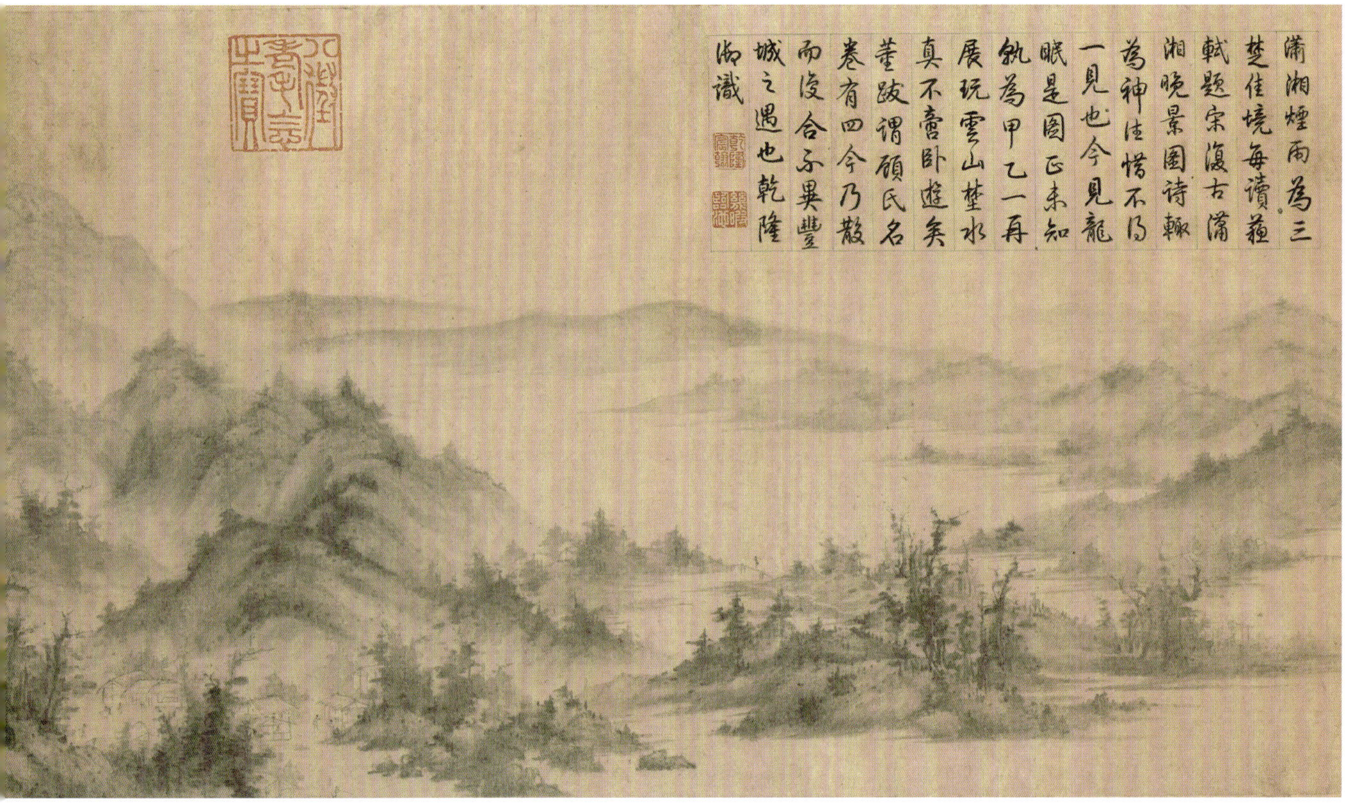
瀟湘煙雨為三楚佳境每讀蘇軾題宋復古瀟湘晚景圖詩輒為神往惜不得一見也今見龍眠是圖正未知孰為甲乙一再展玩雲山楚水真不啻卧遊矣董跋謂顧氏名卷有四今乃散而復合亦異豐城之遇也乾隆御識

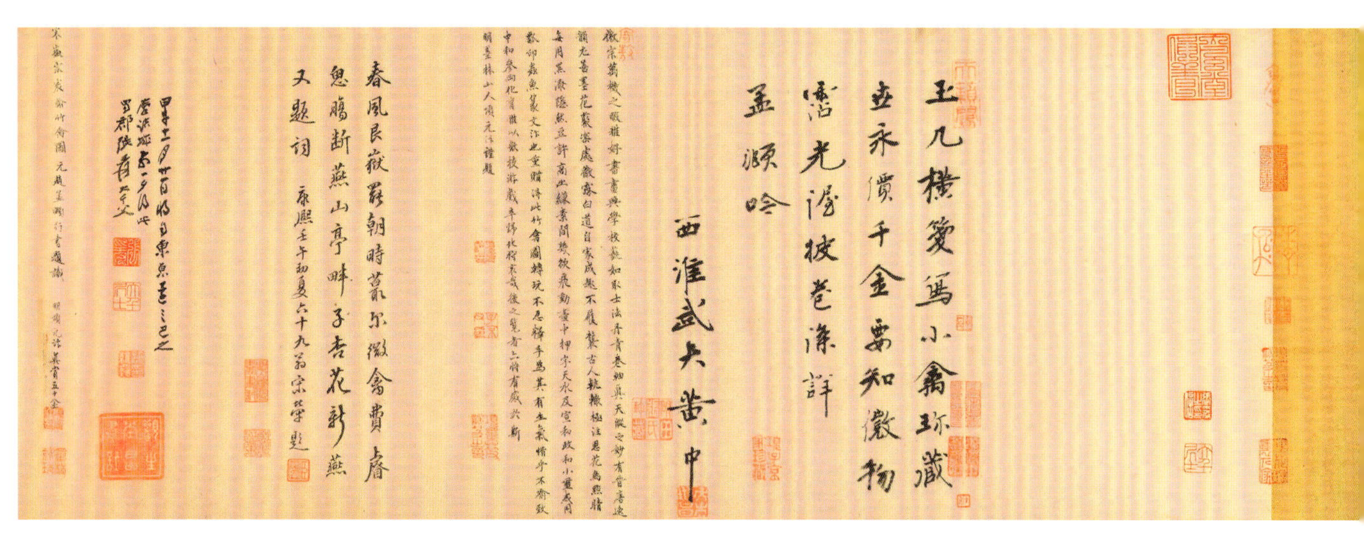

28. 竹禽图

北宋
宋徽宗
绢本设色
手卷
纵33.7、横55.4厘米
大都会艺术博物馆

Finches and Bamboo

Northern Song dynasty (960–1127)
Emperor Huizong
Ink and color on silk
Handscroll
H×W : 33.7×55.4 cm
The Metropolitan Museum of Art
John M. Crawford Jr. Collection, Purchase, Douglas Dillon Gift, 1981

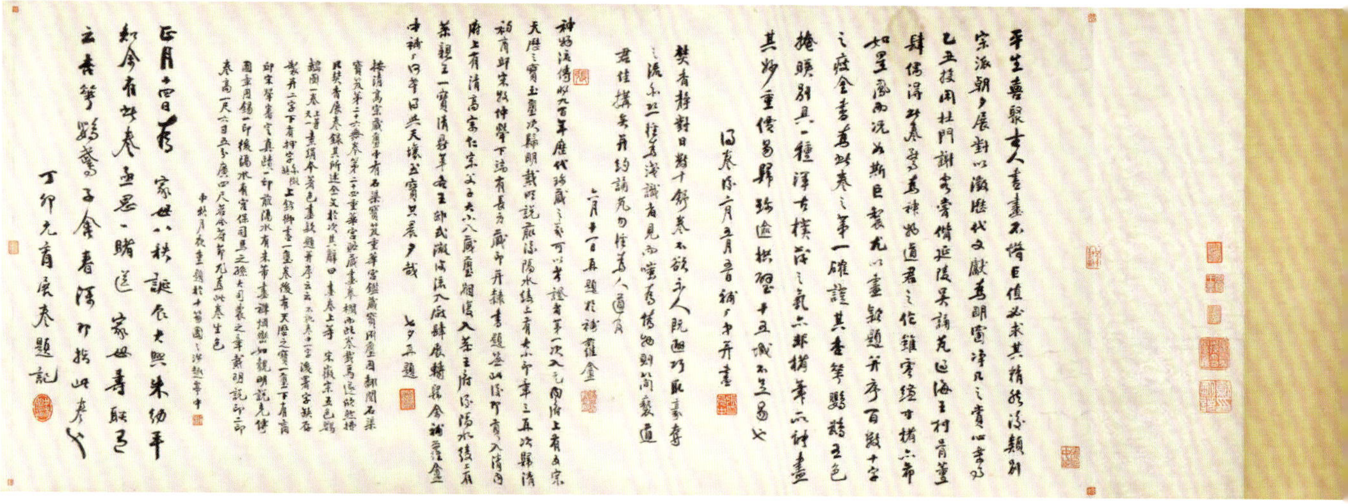

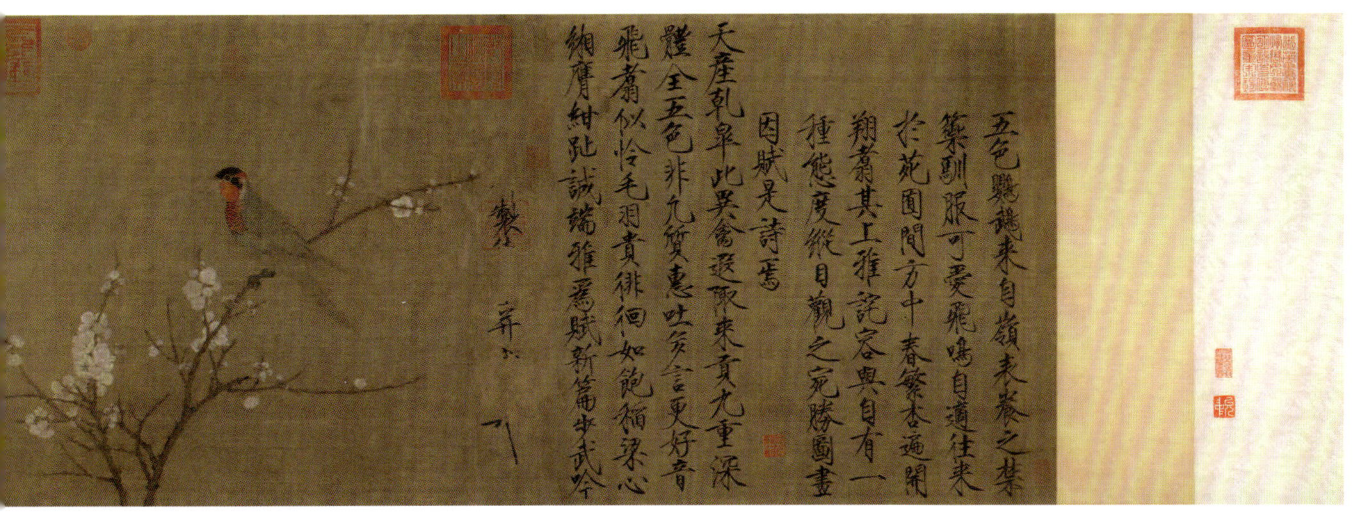

29. 五色鹦鹉图

北宋
宋徽宗
绢本设色
手卷
纵53.3、横125.1厘米
波士顿艺术博物馆

Five-colored Parakeet

Northern Song dynasty (960–1127)
Emperor Huizong
Ink and color on silk
Handscroll
H×W : 53.3×125.1 cm
The Museum of Fine Arts, Boston
Maria Antoinette Evans Fund

五色鸚鵡來自嶺表養之禁
籞馴服可愛飛鳴自適往來
於苑囿間方中春繁杏遍開
翔翥其上雅詫容與自有一
種態度縱目觀之宛勝圖畫
因賦是詩焉
天產乾皐此異禽遐陬來貢九重深
體全五色非凡質惠吐多言更好音
飛翥似憐毛羽貴徘徊如飽稻粱心
緗膺紺趾誠端雅爲賦新篇步武吟

右宣和臨張萱搗練圖明昌以郡望題
籤歟之七璽蓋亦愛之之深乃知嫫母之
姿亦有効其顰者何邪齋郡張紳

金井西風梧桐黃葉慣寫長门詩句斷墨零縑留得墜釵眉嫵
捲羅袖一點砂紅鎖深院守宮譏人間子夜清砧秋窗愁
響搗衣杵　含情都在毫素重見宣和秘殿淡螺描取又過
明昌添寫作半行垂露笑飛來七十九央只相識浣紗溪女更
誰摹天寶宮人花邊聽羯鼓　此卷自丁丑冬題後久未展閱秋八
月拾點藏書賦綺羅香一解立冬後一日天宇晴暖蘿菊盈庭木
瓜香撲鼻味來錯今歲六月大兒舉子頃又叨贊書老母色喜試
御賜松花江研書於金章宗璽紙後宣和畫譜載張萱以金井梧桐
秋葉黃之句寫長門怨甚有思致又羯鼓圖亦萱所畫故辭中及之
余家有萱祈巧圖雅麗絕倫非宣和所可到也
康熙己卯九月十七日江邨高士奇在柘湖簡靜齋

宋徽宗摹張萱搗練畫筆墨超妙後人豈能彷
彿金章宗題籤識以七璽其珎重可知余得此卷
於京師攜歸江村今日裝畢謹跋於後康熙丁丑嘉
平十六日簡靜齋寒窗晴暖曉起擁爐焚沉水展觀
至再試君房墨書藏用老人高士奇

宋徽宗摹唐張萱搗練圖見於松泉老人墨緣彙觀云絹本如新大致
色明昌書標題有張紳一跋與此合又經高江邨收藏前題詞後
再題跋並為題畫而江邨銷夏錄不載此卷者銷夏錄刻於康熙
丙午此跋在康熙己卯年蓋銷夏錄刻成後六年所得前題詞
後云家有萱祈巧圖雅麗絕倫非宣和所可到考萱祈巧圖見銷
夏錄中江邨既藏有萱祈巧圖則摹此畫者其精鑒確可知
又明昌書學宣和瘦金書非宣和御題畫圖宮內八[illegible]明昌書圖今
尚以為可驗而知見於此卷亦其一證也光緒戊戌閏月羅振玉識

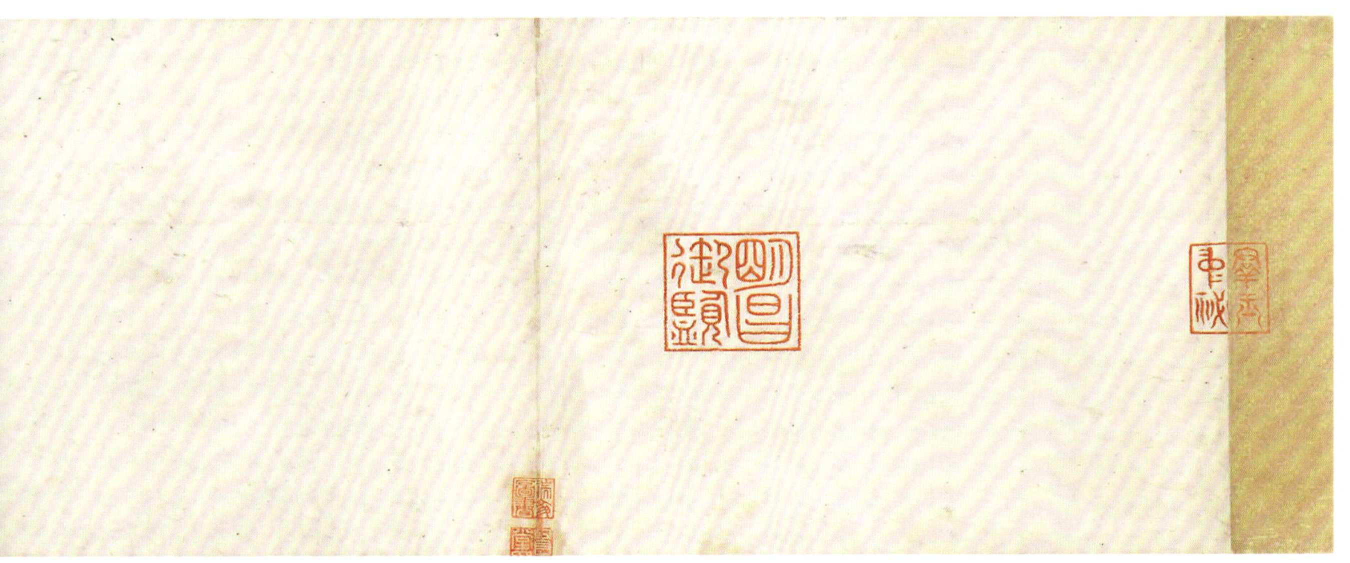

30. 捣练图

北宋
宋徽宗
绢本设色
手卷
纵37.1、横145厘米
波士顿艺术博物馆

Court Ladies Preparing Newly Woven Silk

Northern Song dynasty (960–1127)
Emperor Huizong
Ink and color on silk
Handscroll
H×W : 37.1×145 cm
The Museum of Fine Arts, Boston
Chinese and Japanese Special Fund

31. 荔枝禽鸟图

北宋
（传）宋徽宗
绢本设色
册页
纵22.9、横23.5厘米
大都会艺术博物馆

Bunch of Purple Lychees

Northern Song dynasty (960–1127)
Attributed to Emperor Huizong
Ink and color on silk
Album leaf
H×W : 22.9×23.5 cm
The Metropolitan Museum of Art
John Stewart Kennedy Fund, 1913

32. 冬景山水图

北宋
李公年
绢本设色
立轴
纵129.6、横48.3厘米
普林斯顿大学美术馆

Winter Evening Landscape

Northern Song dynasty (960–1127)
Li Gongnian
Ink and color on silk
Hanging scroll
H×W : 129.6×48.3 cm
The Princeton University Art Museum
Gift of DuBois Schanck Morris, Class of 1893

右東丹王李贊華亦作射鹿
圖按史傳贊華遼太祖之長
子也因光中遜嗣主德光之逼
越海抵登州歸唐明宗因賜姓
李授懷海軍節度使嘗載圖
書自隨好畫挾彈射獵游騎
服用皆纓胡之纓蓋安於所習
故也觀其筆法圓細人馬動健
生有盛唐風韻故可寶也
時至正十二年正月十日李德润題

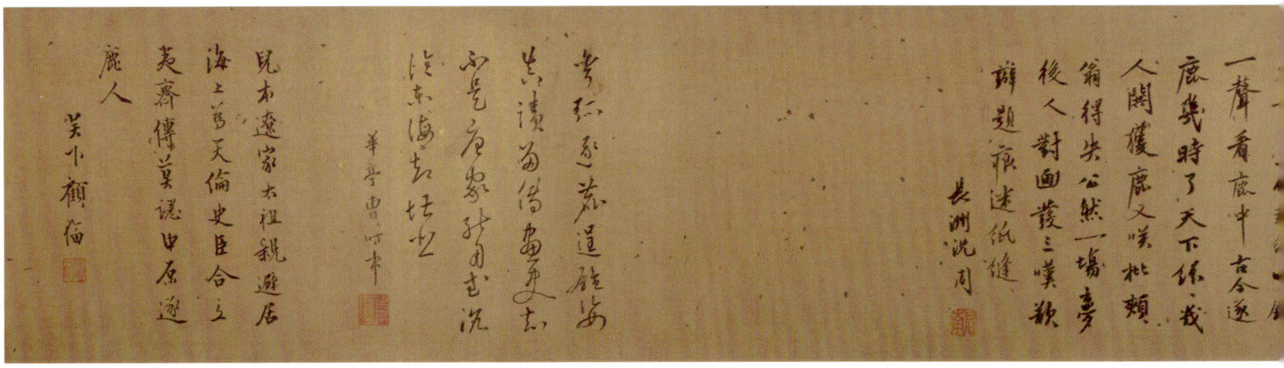
長洲沈周

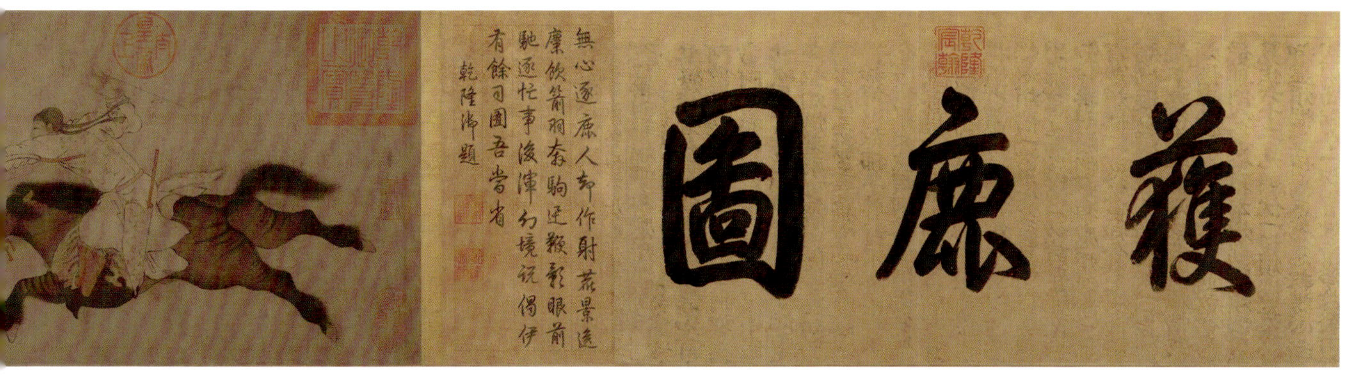

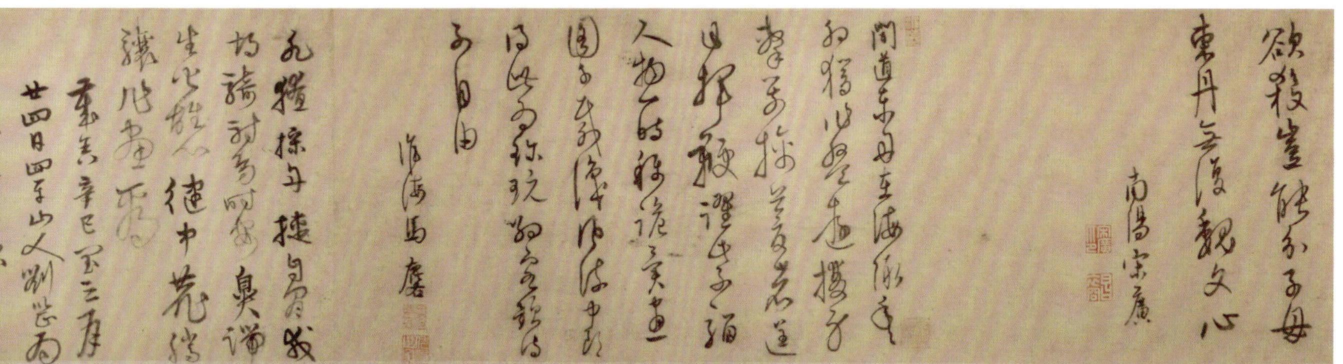

33. 获鹿图

宋或金
（传）黄宗道
纸本设色
手卷
纵24.6、横78.9厘米
大都会艺术博物馆

Stag Hunt

Song dynasty (960–1279) or Jin dynasty (1115–1234)
Attributed to Huang Zongdao
Ink and color on paper
Handscroll
H×W : 24.6×78.9 cm
The Metropolitan Museum of Art
Edward Elliott Family Collection, Purchase, The Dillon Fund Gift, 1982

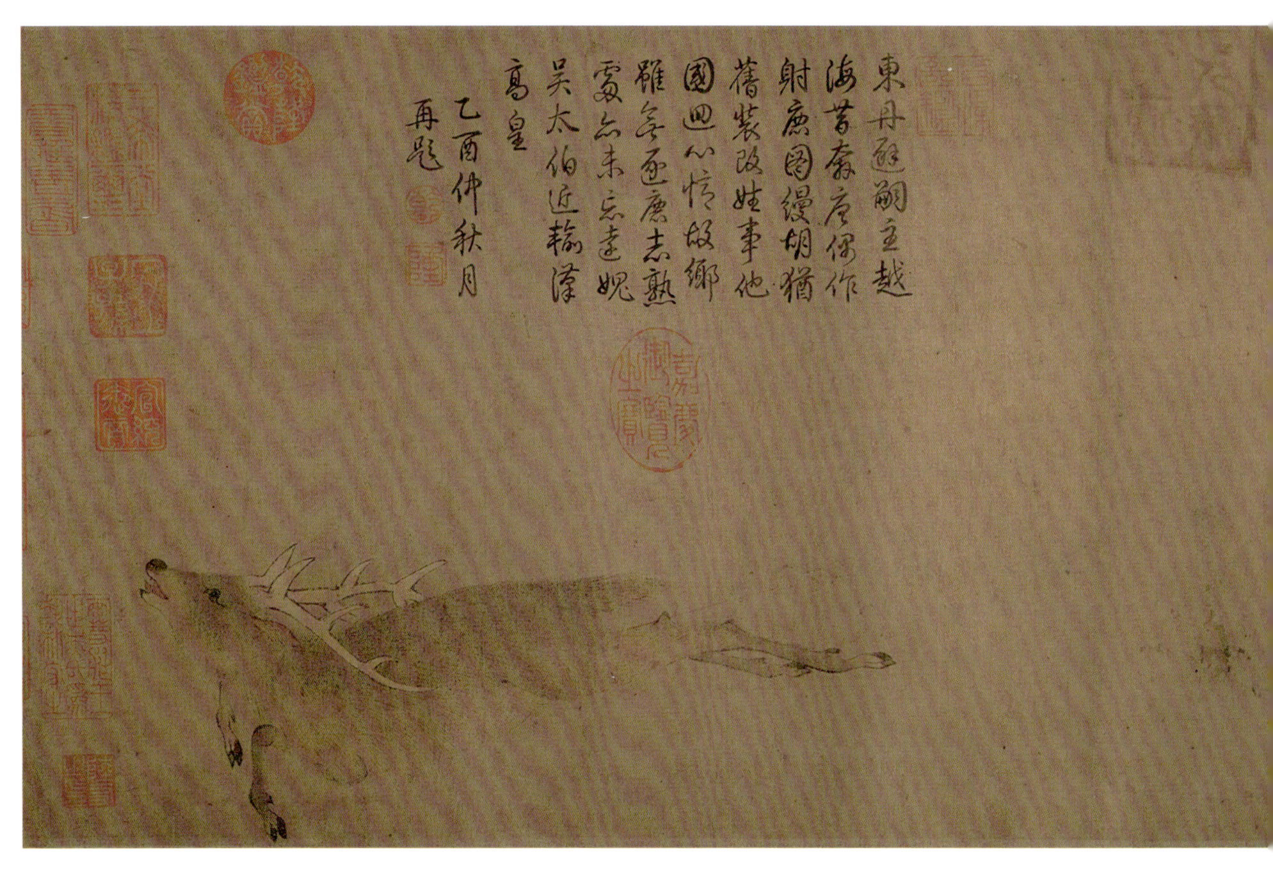

係世數浉迹惜其淪墜乃采國朝傳燈廣燈二錄諸方語要及者老所傳載為一圖謂之正法眼藏宗派叙而銘曰

吾聞如來大光明藏含攝諸法與太虛等吾身吾心天地萬物有識無識有相無相皆吾藏中種種諸寶具正眼者則能照之不具正眼為彼所眩其眩惟何妄見同異或生愛樂或起厭苦流浪輪迴未嘗休止吾藏諸寶化為塵職如來大慈為諸迷途舉示一華以開正眼惟大迦葉默然微笑以是付囑流通敷演菩提達磨初入震旦炳一寶炬分百千燈燈燈煥耀其光如一或示以語或見而叱或鑒而嘆一指三峯四箭五位家毬彎地提之引弓面壁敲狀吹毛指拍行住坐卧歌舞咲哭方圓長短從奪逆順於一毫端現寶王剎以一芥子內須彌山辟如衆流入海不二若有衆生見此一法則諸寶藏咸充受用若有衆生從此悟入則諸大千悉皆銷殞寶無一寶可受用者初如童稚誤認木偶男女老少鬼神諸相不知是妄咸以為真或咲或懼為彼所轉及其長立能認木偶本無實相皆因造作假合成就無不是妄能辨此妄是謂真見法法住位本無還故任從游戲終不再疑不須去妄別生聖解若生聖解即落邪見天高地下日晝月夜稽首如來正法眼藏

泰定二年乙丑五月五日為無可了道人書于平江休休菴枬檀閣下　思退居士郭畀

34. 蕃王礼佛图

北宋
（传）赵光辅
绢本设色
手卷
纵28.6、横103.5厘米
克利夫兰美术馆

Barbarian Royalty Worshiping Buddha

Northern Song dynasty (960–1127)
Attributed to Zhao Guangfu
Ink and color on silk
Handscroll
H×W : 28.6×103.5 cm
The Cleveland Museum of Art
Gift of Severance and Greta Millikin 1957.358

光輔

35. 藻鱼图

北宋
（传）赵克夐
绢本设色
册页
纵22.5、横25.1厘米
大都会艺术博物馆

Fish at Play

Northern Song dynasty (960–1127)
Attributed to Zhao Kexiong
Ink and color on silk
Album leaf
H×W : 22.5×25.1 cm
The Metropolitan Museum of Art
John Stewart Kennedy Fund, 1913

36. 睢阳五老图之朱贯像

北宋
佚名
绢本设色
册页
纵40.3、横32.2厘米
耶鲁大学艺术博物馆

Portrait of Zhu Guan from Set Five Old Men of Suiyang

Northern Song dynasty (960–1127)
Artist unknown
Ink and color on silk
Album leaf
H×W : 40.3×32.2 cm
The Yale University Art Gallery
Hobart and Edward Small Moore Memorial Collection, Gift of Mrs. William H. Moore

37. 睢阳五老图之杜衍像

Portrait of Du Yan from Set Five Old Men of Suiyang

北宋
佚名
绢本设色
册页
纵40.3、横31.4厘米
耶鲁大学艺术博物馆

Northern Song dynasty (960–1127)
Artist unknown
Ink and color on silk
Album leaf
H×W : 40.3×31.4 cm
The Yale University Art Gallery
Hobart and Edward Small Moore Memorial Collection, Gift of Mrs. William H. Moore

38. 睢阳五老图之毕世长像

北宋
佚名
绢本设色
册页
纵40、横32.1厘米
大都会艺术博物馆

Portrait of Bi Shichang from Set Five Old Men of Suiyang

Northern Song dynasty (960–1127)
Artist unknown
Ink and color on silk
Album leaf
H×W : 40×32.1 cm
The Metropolitan Museum of Art
Rogers Fund, 1917

39. 睢阳五老图之王涣像

北宋
佚名
绢本设色
册页
纵41.7、横31.7厘米
弗利尔美术馆

Portrait of Wang Huan from Set Five Old Men of Suiyang

Northern Song dynasty (960–1127)
Artist unknown
Ink and color on silk
Album leaf
H×W : 41.7×31.7 cm
The Freer Gallery of Art
Purchase–Charles Lang Freer Endowment

40. 睢阳五老图之冯平像

北宋
佚名
绢本设色
册页
纵42.3、横32.6厘米
弗利尔美术馆

Portrait of Feng Ping from Set Five Old Men of Suiyang

Northern Song dynasty (960–1127)
Artist unknown
Ink and color on silk
Album leaf
H×W : 42.3×32.6 cm
The Freer Gallery of Art
Purchase–Charles Lang Freer Endowment

41. 乞巧图

Palace Banquet

北宋
佚名
绢本设色
立轴
纵161.6、横110.8厘米
大都会艺术博物馆

Northern Song dynasty (960–1127)
Artist unknown
Ink and color on silk
Hanging scroll
H×W : 161.6×110.8 cm
The Metropolitan Museum of Art
Ex coll.: C. C. Wang Family, Gift of Oscar L. Tang Family, 2010

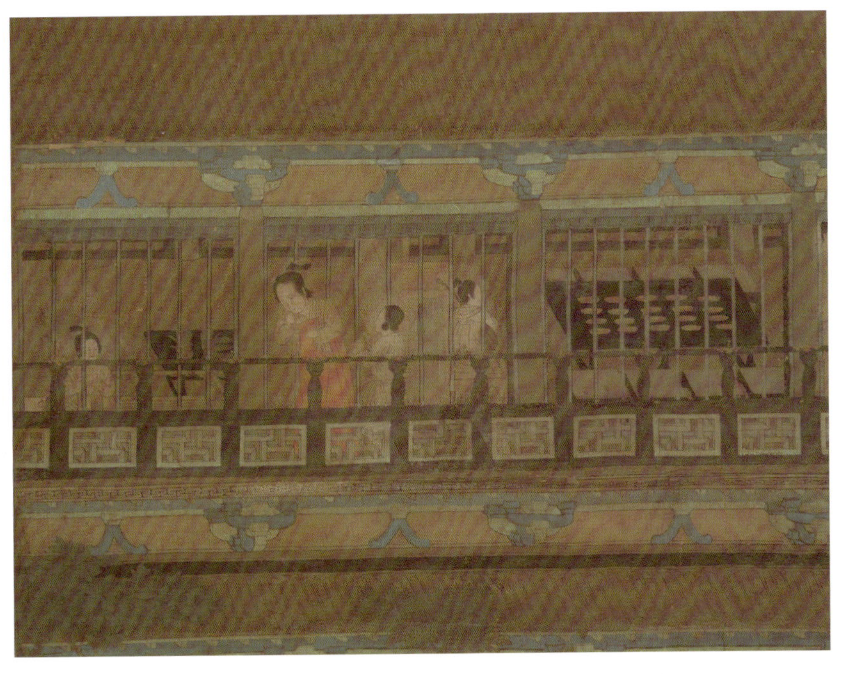

42. 聘金图

金
（传）杨邦基
绢本设色
手卷
纵26.7、横142.2厘米
大都会艺术博物馆

Diplomatic Mission to Jin

Jin dynasty (1115–1234)
Attributed to Yang Bangji
Ink and color on silk
Handscroll
H×W : 26.7×142.2 cm
The Metropolitan Museum of Art
Edward Elliott Family Collection, Purchase, The Dillon Fund Gift, 1982

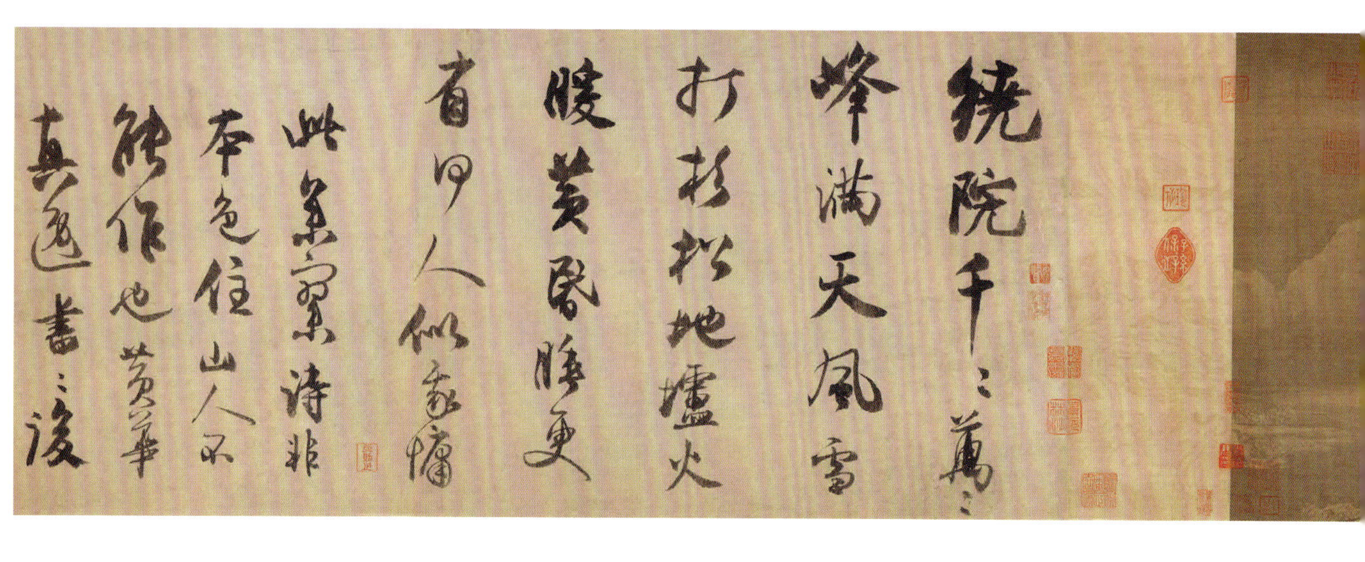
繞院千千萬萬
峰滿天風雪
打杉松地爐火
暖黄昏勝更
有何人似我慵
此某案詩非
本色住山人不
能作也黄華
真迹書之後

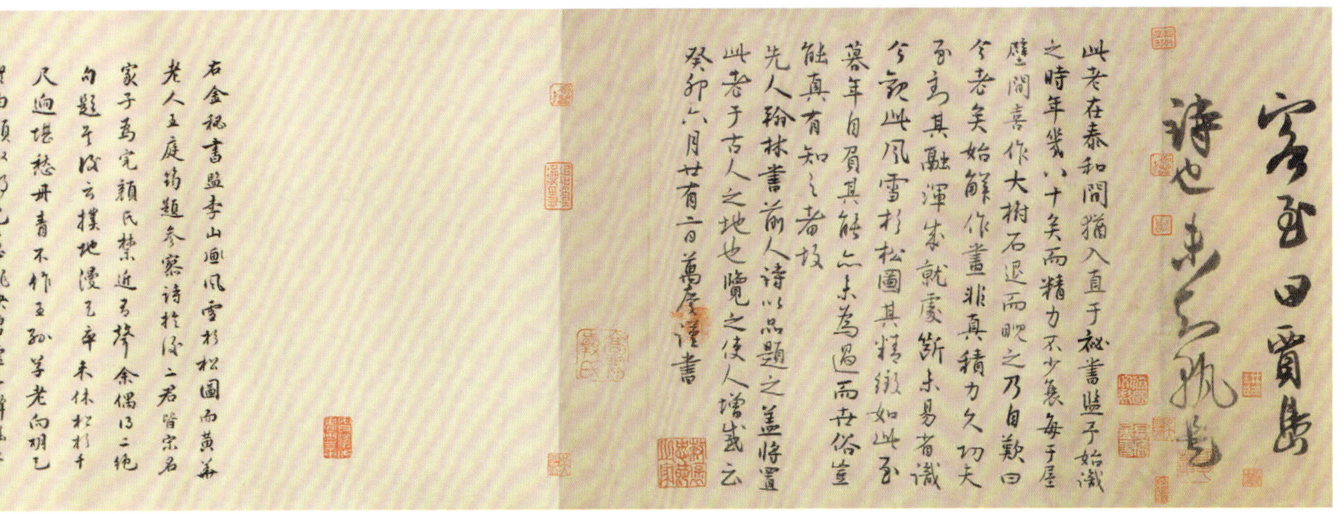

43. 风雪松杉图

金
李山
绢本设色
手卷
纵29.7、横79.3厘米
弗利尔美术馆

Wind and Snow in Fir Pines

Jin dynasty (1115–1234)
Li Shan
Ink and color on silk
Handscroll
H×W : 29.7×79.3 cm
The Freer Gallery of Art
Gift of Eugene and Agnes E. Meyer

平陽李山製

44. 明妃出塞图

Empress Mingfei Crossing Border

金
（传）宫素然
纸本水墨
手卷
纵30.2、横160.2厘米
大阪市立美术馆

Jin dynasty (1115–1234)
Attributed to Gong Suran
Ink on paper
Handscroll
H×W : 30.2×160.2 cm
The Osaka City Museum of Fine Arts

45. 平林霁色图

Clear Weather in Valley

金或元
佚名
纸本设色
手卷
纵37.5、横150.8厘米
波士顿艺术博物馆

Jin dynasty (1115–1234) or Yuan dynasty (1271–1368)
Artist unknown
Ink and color on paper
Handscroll
H×W : 37.5×150.8 cm
The Museum of Fine Arts, Boston
Chinese and Japanese Special Fund

46. 雪中林鸟图

Birds in Grove in Mountainous Winter Landscape

金
（传）高焘
绢本设色
立轴
纵174.9、横90.2厘米
克利夫兰美术馆

Jin dynasty (1115–1234)
Attributed to Gao Tao
Ink and color on silk
Hanging scroll
H×W : 174.9×90.2 cm
The Cleveland Museum of Art
John L. Severance Fund 1966.115

及宋宋襄公贈之以馬二十乘

及楚楚子饗之曰公子若反晉國則何以報不
穀對曰子女玉帛則君有之羽毛齒革則君地
生焉其波及晉國者君之餘也其何以報君曰
雖然何以報我對曰若以君之靈得反晉國晉
楚治兵遇於中原其辟君三舍若不獲命其左
執鞭弭右屬櫜鞬以與君周旋子玉請殺之楚
子曰晉公子廣而儉文而有禮其從者肅而寬
忠而能力晉侯無親外內惡之吾聞姬姓唐叔
之後其後衰者也其將由晉公子乎天將興之
誰能廢之違天必有大咎乃送諸秦

47. 晋文公复国图

南宋
（传）李唐
绢本设色
手卷
纵29.4、横828厘米
大都会艺术博物馆

Duke Wen of Jin Recovering His State

Southern Song dynasty (1127–1279)
Attributed to Li Tang
Ink and color on silk
Handscroll
H×W : 29.4×828 cm
The Metropolitan Museum of Art
Ex coll.: C. C. Wang Family, Gift of The Dillon Fund, 1973

李唐字晞古河陽人在宣靖間已著名畫院南渡後流寓臨安賣畫自給鮮有識者途窮因嘗往謁日嘗裡煙村雨景難看之容易作之難早知不入時人眼多買胭脂畫牡丹可繫見矣後有中使識之奏聞復入待詔之變荒學遂為畫院之首此圖流後有宣和大小璽後人復目為北宋而不知為晞古早年之筆高古洒尔尤足珍也至于高宗書雖丈與晚年書法不同想初駐臨安時流離播遷冀圖復國而登天且見此圖有不驚心感歎者乎乾書登雖有以夫作此訂正而改題洵有據哉

元統二年歲八月既朔石巖題是日

弁陽周公謹同觀

宋高宗萬機之暇喜書經文嘗曰寫字當寫經書不惟學字又得經書不忘曾寫有十三經刻石禁中迨元初楊璉真伽發宋諸陵造塔取故經石為塔址遂散落如雲煙矣予所見真蹟惟毛詩頗多每十篇作一卷虛其左令馬和之補圖大抵乃德壽宮事此卷則李畫在前人物類伯時樹石宮宇肖黃筌較勝晚年之作而書在後者蓋證為思陵早年筆有虞永興風規是稱二絕

成化六年四月望日吳寬題

六如生周子球觀

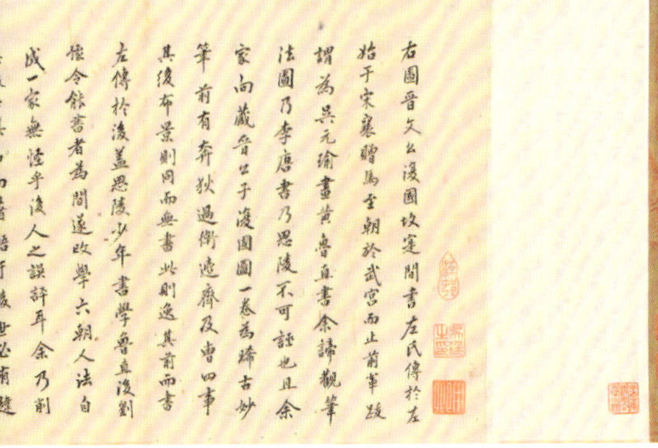

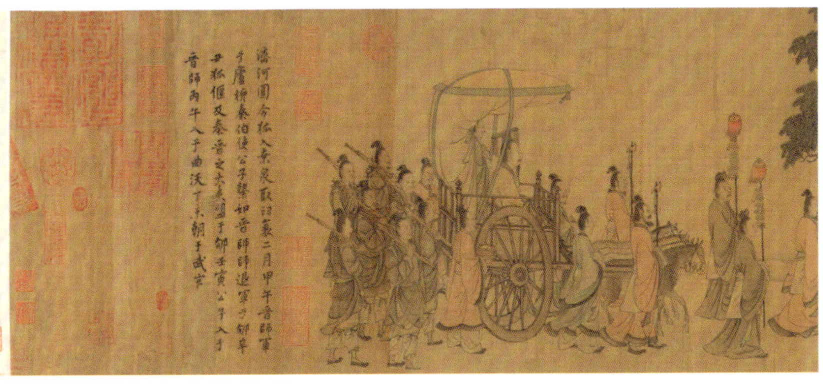

48. 远岫晴云图

Clouds on Clear Day Around Distant Peaks

南宋绍兴四年（公元1134年）
米友仁
纸本水墨
立轴
纵24.7、横28.6厘米
大阪市立美术馆

Southern Song dynasty (1127–1279), dated 1134
Mi Youren
Ink on paper
Hanging scroll
H×W : 24.7×28.6 cm
The Osaka City Museum of Fine Arts

米元暉畫大似二王書字有無形
而無拘礙偶逢中達村墅雲山之
勝就筆漬紙歸以獻
宸扆旋復賜當代迄兹今為予几
格嗚呼人俱非矣物仍存焉敬當
寶惜以傳無窮慶元庚申初伏日
琅琊默菴聖與志

說詩者云書意十分之詩三
分而其理雅予於畫亦云蓋
工人之畫往往命意而出於
形似至於高人逸士寄興於是
二者之很也……此帝著

庖丁解牛奏刀騞然協桑林之
舞中經首之會天機流動有不知
其然而然者寧獨庖之於解也為
然耶伯昏氏之於射也秦豆氏之
於馭也亦然觀元暉之於畫也始
知莊列前所云者非但寓言特發
揮夫天機流動之不可遏焉耳
煙水雲山皆夢畫筠疎林古木
皆無畫譜興酣一揮千里之遠
萃乎咫尺安得醉李永歌之醉
顛疾書之手左方以成夫三絶之
妙也夫
正統戊子蕤賓節金陵宋[illegible]拜手書

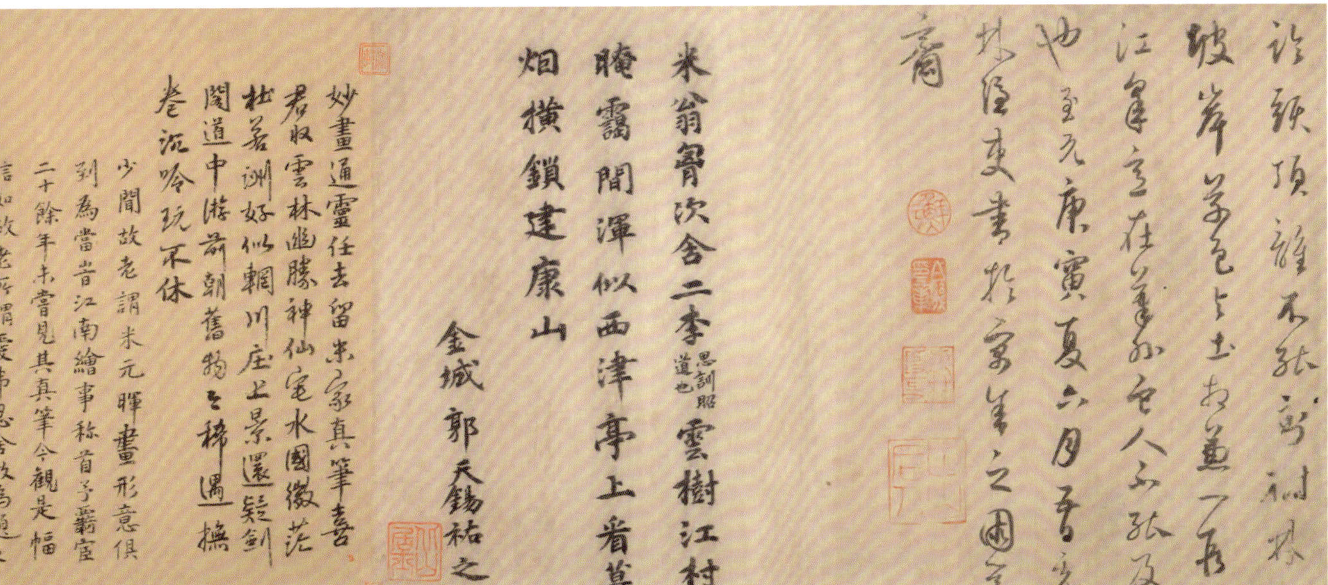

49. 云山图

南宋
（传）米友仁
纸本水墨
手卷
纵27.6、横57厘米
大都会艺术博物馆

Cloudy Mountains

Southern Song dynasty (1127–1279)
Attributed to Mi Youren
Ink on paper
Handscroll
H×W : 27.6×57 cm
The Metropolitan Museum of Art
Ex coll.: C. C. Wang Family, Purchase, Gift of J. Pierpont Morgan, by exchange, 1973

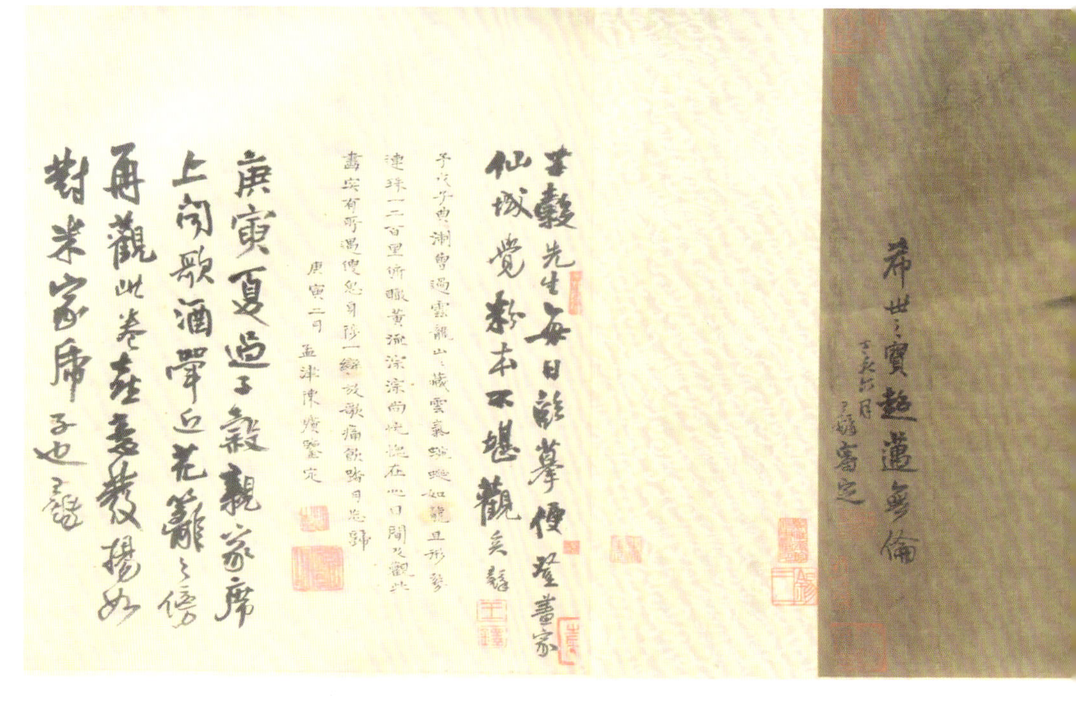

50. 云山图

南宋

（传）米友仁

绢本设色

手卷

纵43.7、横192.6厘米

克利夫兰美术馆

Cloudy Mountains

Southern Song dynasty (1127–1279)

Attributed to Mi Youren

Ink and color on silk

Handscroll

H×W : 43.7×192.6 cm

The Cleveland Museum of Art

Purchase from the J. H. Wade Fund

1933.220

右米友仁畫紙長工部尺二尺三
寸四分高五寸七分山色溟濛烟蘇
晻藹瓦屋五間爲蘇所蔽僅露
屋脊後有宋夏觀下蓋白雲山
舍白文方印錢惟善題下蓋思汲
朱文方印貫㣈爽印前有季振
宜印朱文方印滄葦朱文方印
下今之鑒定朱文長印後有今
之清玩朱文方印雲卿白文方
印述韓甫白文方印平石癖
廖宇文公諒覲于别紙平石之
印曰契此里人公諒之印曰字
文子貞子貞印似印而加蓋者
前有式古堂書畫朱文長印
遂有今之朱文方印仙客朱文
方印與書畫彙考所載合惟
彙考稱長二尺二寸高五寸微有
不同余所用乃工部營造尺十可
用疑是裁衣尺故有參差耳
張米菴謂高米水墨雲山皆
數十百次積累而成非遂人草
草點染所可同類而觀此畫
純用濃墨層層點染斷非元以
後人所能小米雖無覲字印記
而元人平石無夢子貞三家
皆定爲米畫又經莫雲卿
季滄葦卞令之三家鑒定今
之又收入彙考可信其爲真迹
也公諒字子貞湖州人元史有
傳平石無夢二人俟考
光緒庚寅陸心源剛父識
門人李延适書

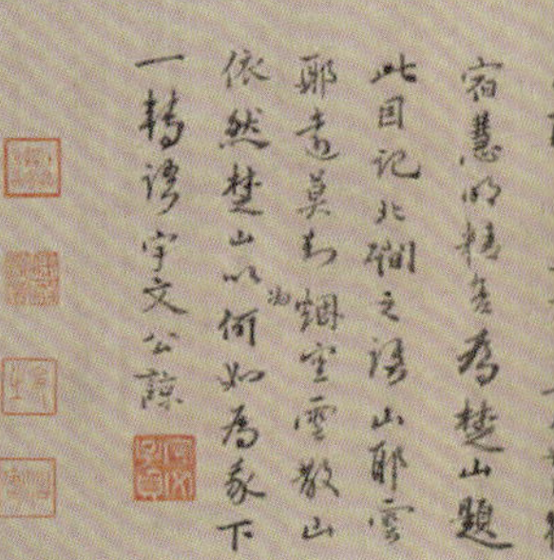

140

51. 云木夏寒图

南宋
（传）米友仁
纸本水墨
手卷
纵18.3、横107.2厘米
耶鲁大学艺术博物馆

Cloudy Woods, Summer Chill

Southern Song dynasty (1127–1279)
Attributed to Mi Youren
Ink on paper
Handscroll
H×W : 18.3×107.2 cm
The Yale University Art Gallery
Hobart and Edward Small Moore Memorial Collection, Gift of Mrs. William H. Moore

52. 婴戏图

南宋
（传）苏汉臣
绢本设色
册页
纵22.7、横25厘米
波士顿艺术博物馆

Children Playing with Balance Toy

Southern Song dynasty (1127–1279)
Attributed to Su Hanchen
Ink and color on silk
Album leaf
H×W : 22.7×25 cm
The Museum of Fine Arts, Boston
John Ware Willard Fund

53. 货郎婴戏图

南宋
（传）苏汉臣
绢本设色
册页
纵26.4、横26.7厘米
大都会艺术博物馆

Knickknack Peddler

Southern Song dynasty (1127–1279)
Attributed to Su Hanchen
Ink and color on silk
Album leaf
H×W : 26.4×26.7 cm
The Metropolitan Museum of Art
Ex coll.: C. C. Wang Family, Purchase, Gift of J. Pierpont Morgan, by exchange, 1973

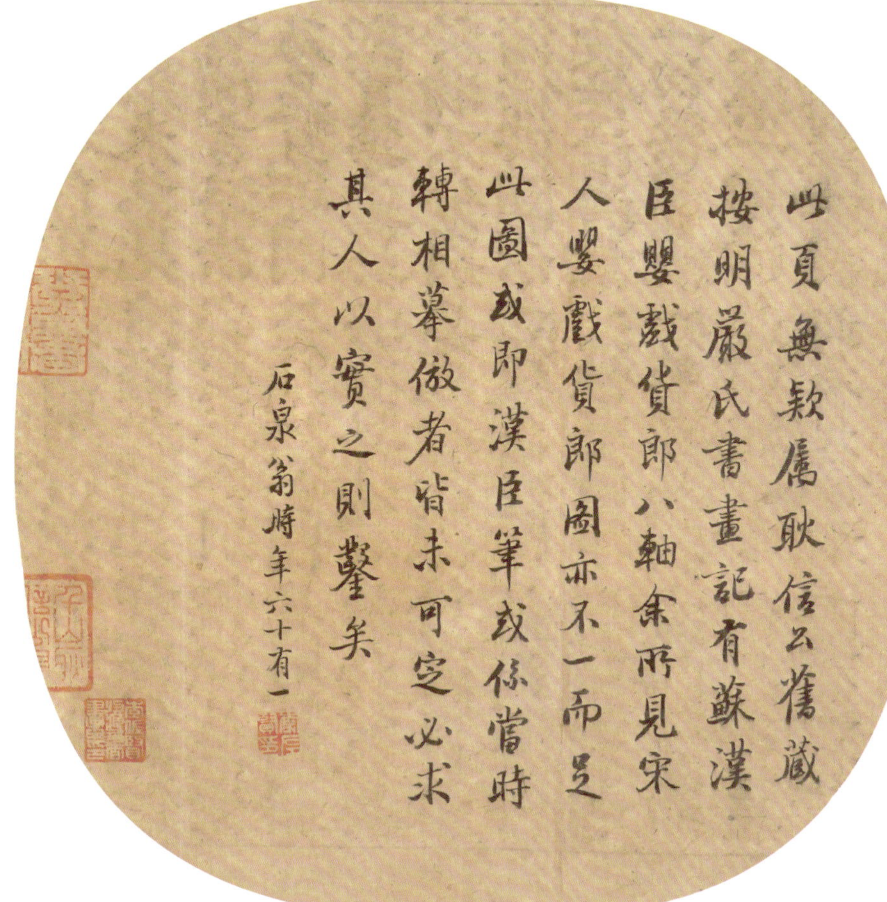
此頁無款屬耿信公舊藏
按明嚴氏書畫記有蘇漢
臣嬰戲貨郎八軸余所見宋
人嬰戲貨郎圖亦不一而足
此圖或即漢臣筆或係當時
轉相摹倣者皆未可定必求
其人以實之則鑿矣
石泉翁時年六十有一

54. 红白芙蓉图

南宋庆元三年（公元1197年）
李迪
绢本设色
册页
每开：纵25.2、横25.5厘米
东京国立博物馆

Red and White Hibiscuses

Southern Song dynasty (1127–1279), dated 1197
Li Di
Ink and color on silk
Album leaf
H×W(each leaf) : 25.2×25.5 cm
The Tokyo National Museum
ColBase(https://colbase.nich.go.jp/collection_items/tnm/TA-137?locale=ja)

55. 古木竹禽图

南宋
李迪
绢本设色
册页
纵24.8、横26.1厘米
克利夫兰美术馆

Birds on Tree above Cataract

Southern Song dynasty (1127–1279)
Li Di
Ink and color on silk
Album leaf
H×W : 24.8×26.1 cm
The Cleveland Museum of Art
Gift of Mrs. A. Dean Perry 1964.155

56. 竹虫图

南宋
吴炳
绢本设色
册页
纵24.8、横26.8厘米
克利夫兰美术馆

Bamboo and Insects

Southern Song dynasty (1127–1279)
Wu Bing
Ink and color on silk
Album leaf
H×W : 24.8×26.8 cm
The Cleveland Museum of Art
Gift of Mrs. A. Dean Perry 1964.154

57. 仿高克明溪山雪意图

南宋
（传）刘松年
绢本设色
手卷
纵41.6、横241.3厘米
大都会艺术博物馆

Streams and Mountains Under Fresh Snow After Gao Keming

Southern Song dynasty (1127–1279)
Attributed to Liu Songnian
Ink and color on silk
Handscroll
H×W : 41.6×241.3 cm
The Metropolitan Museum of Art
Gift of John M. Crawford Jr., 1984

58. 听琴图

南宋
（传）刘松年
绢本设色
册页
纵23.8、横24.6厘米
克利夫兰美术馆

Listening to Qin

Southern Song dynasty (1127–1279)
Attributed to Liu Songnian
Ink and color on silk
Album leaf
H×W : 23.8×24.6 cm
The Cleveland Museum of Art
Leonard C. Hanna, Jr. Fund 1983.85

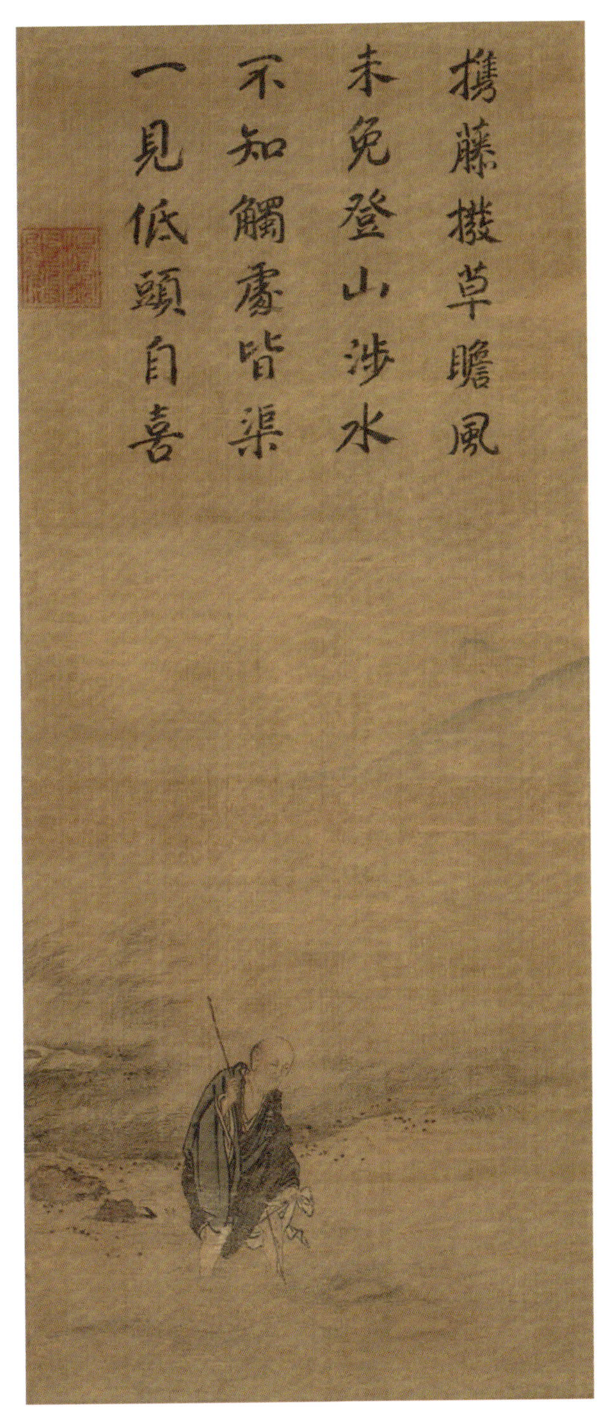

59. 洞山渡水图

南宋
马远
绢本设色
立轴
纵77.6、横33厘米
东京国立博物馆

Priest Dongshan Wading Stream

Southern Song dynasty (1127–1279)
Ma Yuan
Ink and color on silk
Hanging scroll
H×W : 77.6×33 cm
The Tokyo National Museum
ColBase(https://colbase.nich.go.jp/collection_items/tnm/TA-138?locale=ja)

60. 寒江独钓图

Solitary Angler on Wintery River

南宋
马远
绢本设色
手卷
纵26.7、横50.6厘米
东京国立博物馆

Southern Song dynasty (1127–1279)
Ma Yuan
Ink and color on silk
Handscroll
H×W : 26.7×50.6 cm
The Tokyo National Museum
ColBase(https://colbase.nich.go.jp/collection_items/tnm/TA-140?locale=ja)

61. 水溪竹禽图

南宋
马远
绢本设色
立轴
纵61、横37厘米
克利夫兰美术馆

Bamboo and Ducks by Rushing Stream

Southern Song dynasty (1127–1279)
Ma Yuan
Ink and color on silk
Hanging scroll
H×W : 61×37 cm
The Cleveland Museum of Art
Purchase from the J. H. Wade Fund 1967.145

62. 高士观瀑图

南宋
马远
绢本设色
册页
纵25.1、横26厘米
大都会艺术博物馆

Scholar Viewing Waterfall

Southern Song dynasty (1127–1279)
Ma Yuan
Ink and color on silk
Album leaf
H×W : 25.1×26 cm
The Metropolitan Museum of Art
Ex coll.: C. C. Wang Family, Gift of The Dillon Fund, 1973

63. 举杯邀月图

南宋
马远
绢本设色
册页
纵24.5、横25厘米
克利夫兰美术馆

Drinking in Moonlight

Southern Song dynasty (1127–1279)
Ma Yuan
Ink and color on silk
Album leaf
H×W : 24.5×25 cm
The Cleveland Museum of Art
Bequest of Mrs. A. Dean Perry 1997.89

64. 松溪观鹿图

Watching Deer by Pine Shaded Stream

南宋
马远
绢本设色
册页
纵33.7、横39.3厘米
克利夫兰美术馆

Southern Song dynasty (1127–1279)
Ma Yuan
Ink and color on silk
Album leaf
H×W : 33.7×39.3 cm
The Cleveland Museum of Art
Bequest of Mrs. A. Dean Perry 1997.88

65. 月下观梅图

南宋
马远
绢本设色
册页
纵25.1、横26.7厘米
大都会艺术博物馆

Viewing Plum Blossoms by Moonlight

Southern Song dynasty (1127–1279)
Ma Yuan
Ink and color on silk
Album leaf
H×W : 25.1×26.7 cm
The Metropolitan Museum of Art
Gift of John M. Crawford Jr., in honor of Alfreda Murck, 1986

馬遠松陰玩月

66. 松荫玩月图

南宋
（传）马远
绢本设色
册页
纵25.4、横25.4厘米
大都会艺术博物馆

Viewing Moon Under Pine Tree

Southern Song dynasty (1127–1279)
Attributed to Ma Yuan
Ink and color on silk
Album leaf
H×W : 25.4×25.4 cm
The Metropolitan Museum of Art
Bequest of Mrs. A. Dean Perry 1997.89

67. 古松楼阁图

南宋
（传）马远
绢本设色
册页
纵24、横24.7厘米
大阪市立美术馆

Old Pine and Pavilion

Southern Song dynasty (1127–1279)
Attributed to Ma Yuan
Ink and color on silk
Album leaf
H×W : 24×24.7 cm
The Osaka City Museum of Fine Arts

68. 溪山烟霭图

宋或元
（传）江参
绢本水墨
团扇
纵24.2、横26.2厘米
波士顿艺术博物馆

Evening Mist over Valley

Song dynasty (960–1279) or Yuan dynasty (1271–1368)
Attributed to Jiang Shen
Ink on silk
Round fan
H×W : 24.2×26.2 cm
The Museum of Fine Arts, Boston
Denman Waldo Ross Collection

69. 烟村秋霭图

北宋
（传）李安忠
绢本设色
册页
纵24.2、横26.3厘米
克利夫兰美术馆

Cottages in Misty Grove in Autumn

Northern Song dynasty (960–1127)
Attributed to Li Anzhong
Ink and color on silk
Album leaf
H×W : 24.2×26.3 cm
The Cleveland Museum of Art
Gift of Mr. and Mrs. Severance A. Millikin
1963.588

70. 潇湘八景图

南宋
王洪
绢本设色
手卷
每卷：纵23.4、横90.7厘米
普林斯顿大学美术馆

Eight Views of Xiaoxiang Rivers

Southern Song dynasty (1127–1279)
Wang Hong
Ink and color on silk
Handscroll
H×W（each scroll）: 23.4×90.7 cm
The Princeton University Art Museum
Edward L. Elliott Family Collection. Museum purchase, Fowler McCormick, Class of 1921, Fund

71. 货郎图

南宋嘉定五年（公元1212年）
李嵩
绢本设色
册页
纵24.1、横26厘米
克利夫兰美术馆

Knickknack Peddler

Southern Song dynasty (1127–1279), dated 1212
Li Song
Ink and color on silk
Album leaf
H×W : 24.1×26 cm
The Cleveland Museum of Art
Andrew R. and Martha Holden Jennings Fund
1963.582

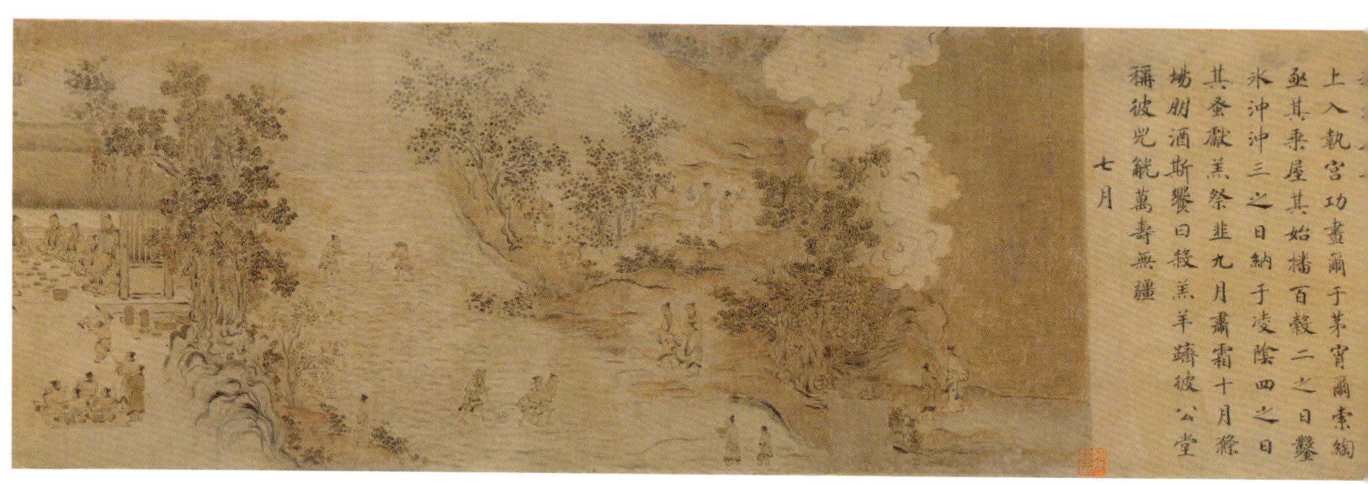
上入執宮功晝爾于茅宵爾索綯
亟其乘屋其始播百穀二之日鑿
冰沖沖三之日納于凌陰四之日
其蚤獻羔祭韭九月肅霜十月滌
場朋酒斯饗曰殺羔羊躋彼公堂
稱彼兕觥萬壽無疆
七月

而歸勞歸士大夫美之故作是詩
也一章言其完也二章言其思也
三章言其室家之望女也四章樂
男女之得及時也君子之於人序
其情而閔其勞所以說也說以使
民民忘其死其唯東山乎我徂東
山慆慆不歸我來自東零雨其濛
我東曰歸我心西悲制彼裳衣勿
士行枚蜎蜎者蠋烝在桑野敦彼
獨宿亦在車下我徂東山慆慆不
歸我來自東零雨其濛果臝之實
亦施于宇伊威在室蠨蛸在戶町
畽鹿場熠燿宵行不可畏也伊可
懷也我徂東山慆慆不歸我來自
東零雨其濛鸛鳴于垤婦歎于室
洒埽穹窒我征聿至有敦瓜苦烝
在栗薪自我不見于今三年我徂
東山慆慆不歸我來自東零雨其
濛倉庚于飛熠燿其羽之子于歸
皇駁其馬親結其縭九十其儀其
新孔嘉其舊如之何
東山

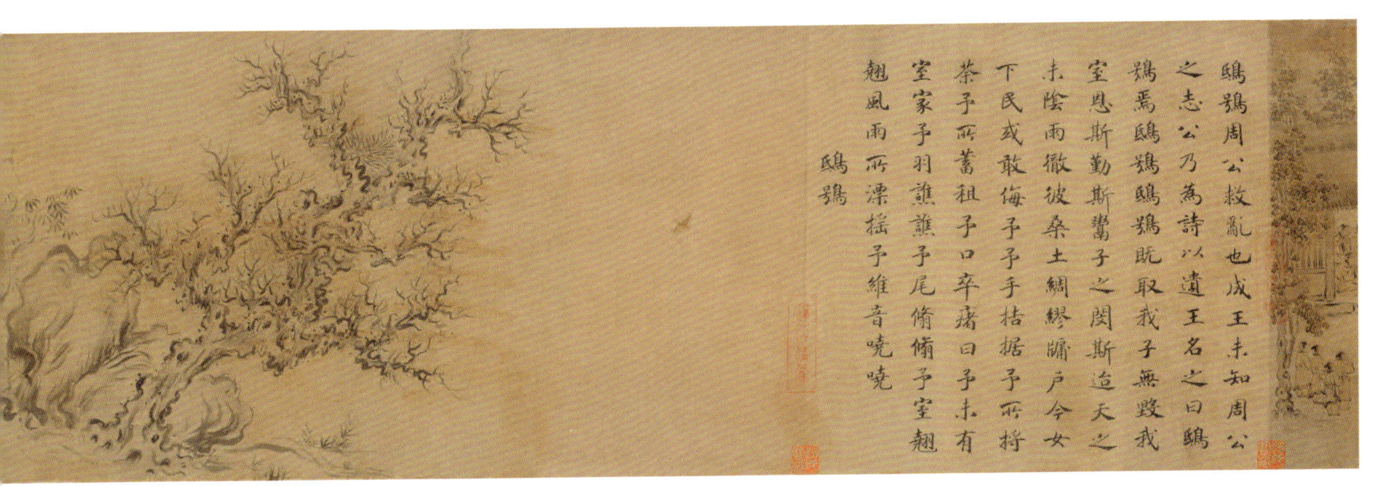

72. 诗经·豳风·七月图

南宋
（传）马和之
绢本设色
手卷
纵27.8、横663.6厘米
大都会艺术博物馆

Illustrations of "Seventh Month" from Odes of Bin

Southern Song dynasty (1127–1279)
Attributed to Ma Hezhi
Ink and color on silk
Handscroll
H×W : 27.8×663.6 cm
The Metropolitan Museum of Art
Ex coll.: C. C. Wang Family, Purchase, Gift of J. Pierpont Morgan, by exchange, 1973

伐柯美周公也周大夫刺朝廷之
不知也伐柯如何匪斧不克取妻
如何匪媒不得伐柯伐柯其則不
遠我覯之子籩豆有踐
伐柯
九罭美周公也周大夫刺朝廷之
不知也九罭之魚鱒魴我覯之子

豳國七篇

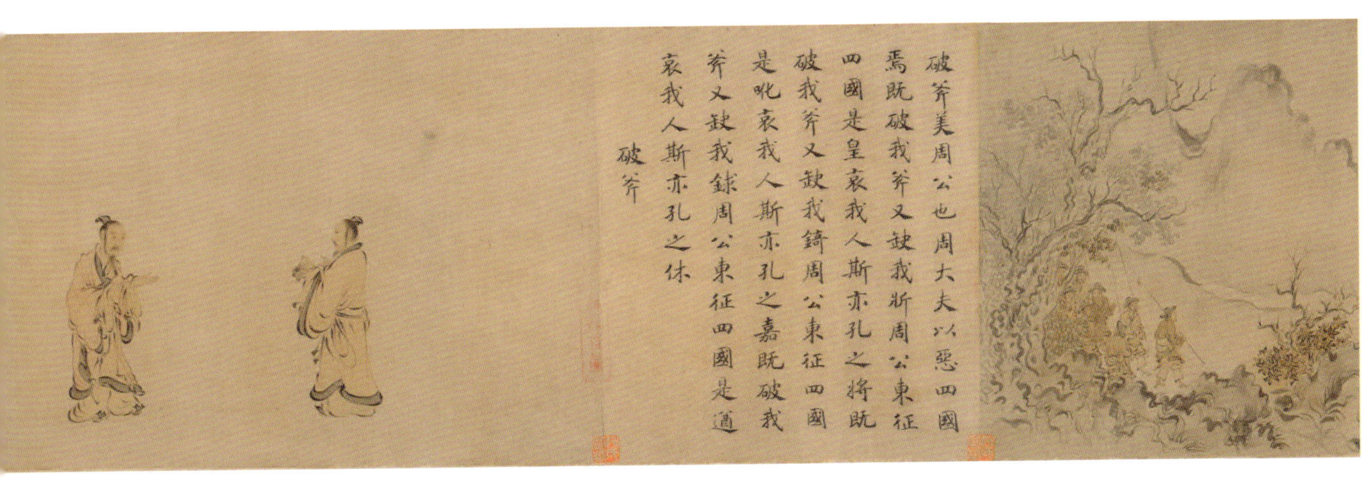
破斧美周公也周大夫以惡四國
焉既破我斧又缺我斨周公東征
四國是皇哀我人斯亦孔之將既
破我斧又缺我錡周公東征四國
是吪哀我人斯亦孔之嘉既破我
斧又缺我銶周公東征四國是遒
哀我人斯亦孔之休
破斧

衮衣繡裳鴻飛遵渚公歸無所於
女信處鴻飛遵陸公歸不復於女
信宿是以有衮衣兮無以我公歸
兮無使我心悲兮
九罭
狼跋美周公也周公攝政遠則四
國流言近則王不知周大夫美其
不失其聖也狼跋其胡載疐其尾
公孫碩膚赤舄几几狼疐其尾載
跋其胡公孫碩膚德音不瑕

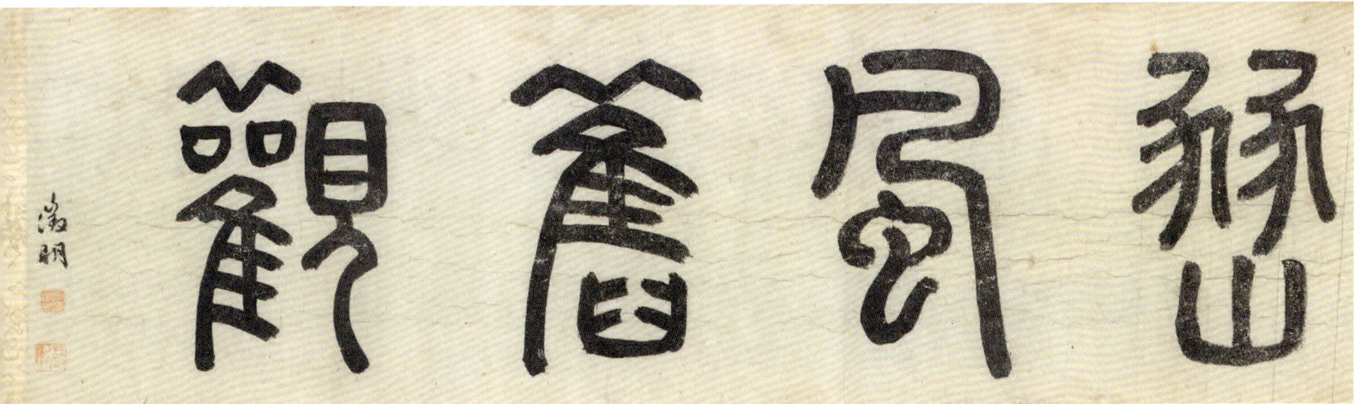

73. 诗经·豳风·七月图

南宋
（传）马和之
纸本水墨
手卷
纵28.8、横436.2厘米
弗利尔美术馆

Illustrations of "Seventh Month" from Odes of Bin

Southern Song dynasty (1127–1279)
Attributed to Ma Hezhi
Ink on paper
Handscroll
H×W : 28.8×436.2 cm
The Freer Gallery of Art
Gift of Charles Lang Freer

皆用青而無水墨其前後之
高宗御書惟此卷獨不設
色而筆法清真古淡另留
蕭閒逸之趣盡遊人以勤儉
開國若姬公之屬稱述於此
和之欲深得詩意不當以無
粉黛點染其真故遂作此
水墨三昧耶西子淡妝勝
於濃抹觀者應有所鑒矣

王穉登題

右宋馬和之豳風七月篇八圖水墨畫和之畫師吳
道元善用掣筆此卷筆意清掣氣韻生動衣摺和暢
有流水行雲之妙草樹飄逸有迴風舞雪之觀雖精
工不及龍眠而於野田蕭疏之景農家作苦之勤情
景畢具理趣無涯昔思陵愛其畫每書毛詩盡其後
令和之為圖此卷各段前均書經文數句未知為思
陵筆否惟第二段乃繪三章取彼斧斯以伐遠揚之
義而所書經文則首章末數句與畫不洽筆蹟亦與
前後不同想此條失去經後人補書未及細審耳八
幅幹縫有金章宗羣玉中秘朱文大印是曾入金內
府者歸尾有文衡山王伯穀二跋古雅可誦文書得
智永筆法王書有率更遺意并首文待詔篆豳風舊
觀四字尤清勁入妙置諸吳興千文中未易伯仲時
咸豐四年春仲書於宣武城南之餘蔭軒張錫庚題

古人圖畫必有所勸戒而作
此馬和之寫豳風七月詩八
幅凡稼穡田桑蠶績之事
莫不纖悉備具雖不設色
而意態自足定非和之不
能作也昔之序詩者云周
公陳王業以告成王謂民
之艱苦者莫甚於農有
國有家者宜思憫之憫之安
之故作是詩備述其艱難
今觀和之此圖蓋生於周
而又於豳古風宛然也校
諸徒丹青以為耳目玩
者豈可同日語哉嘉靖
乙卯春徵明題時年八十
有六

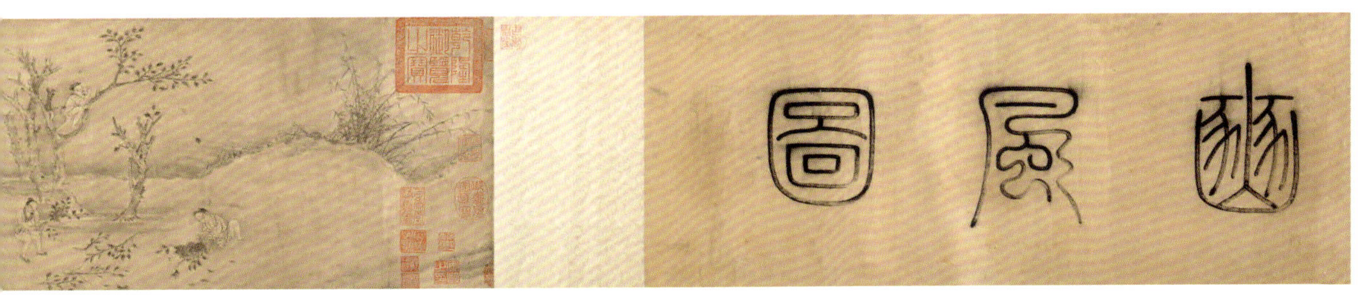

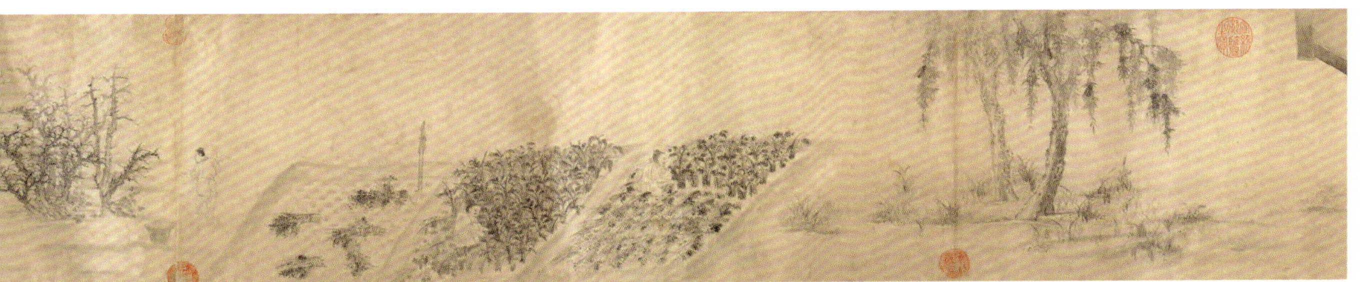

74. 诗经·豳风·七月图

南宋
（传）马和之
纸本水墨
手卷
纵29.2、横1398.9厘米
大都会艺术博物馆

Illustrations of "Seventh Month" from Odes of Bin

Southern Song dynasty (1127–1279)
Attributed to Ma Hezhi
Ink on paper
Handscroll
H×W : 29.2×1398.9 cm
The Metropolitan Museum of Art
John M. Crawford Jr. Collection, Gift of The Dillon Fund, 1982

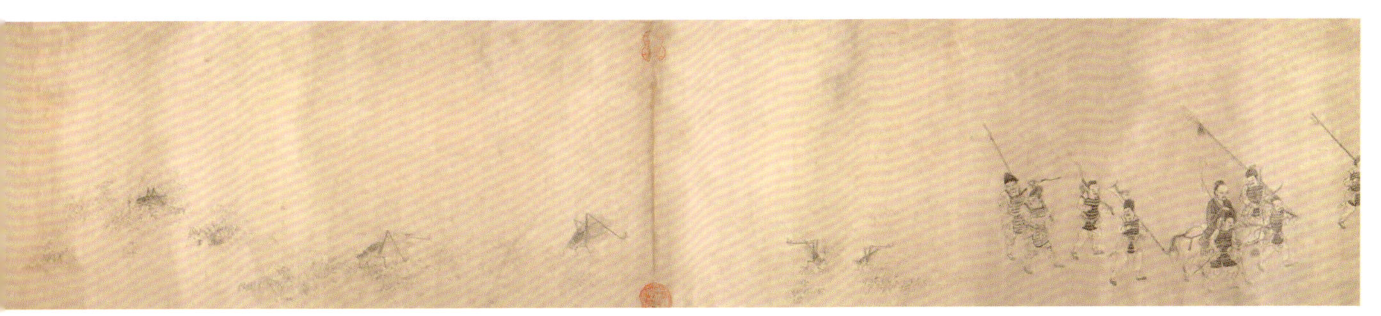

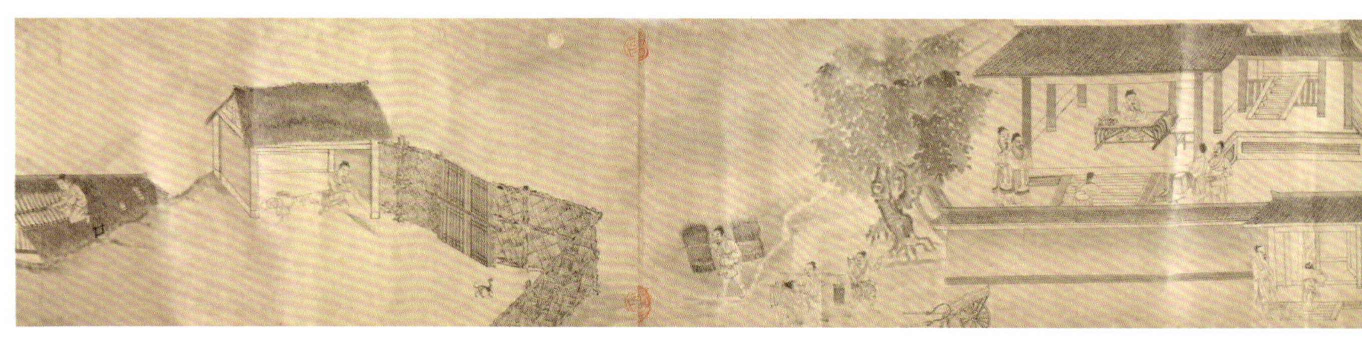

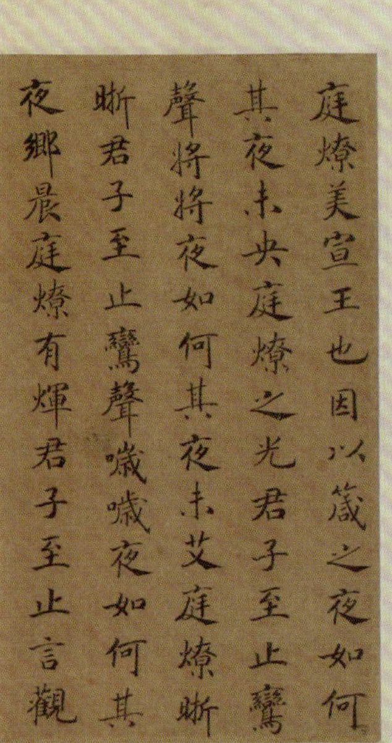
庭燎美宣王也因以箴之夜如何
其夜未央庭燎之光君子至止鸞
聲將將夜如何其夜未艾庭燎晣
晣君子至止鸞聲噦噦夜如何其
夜鄉晨庭燎有煇君子至止言觀

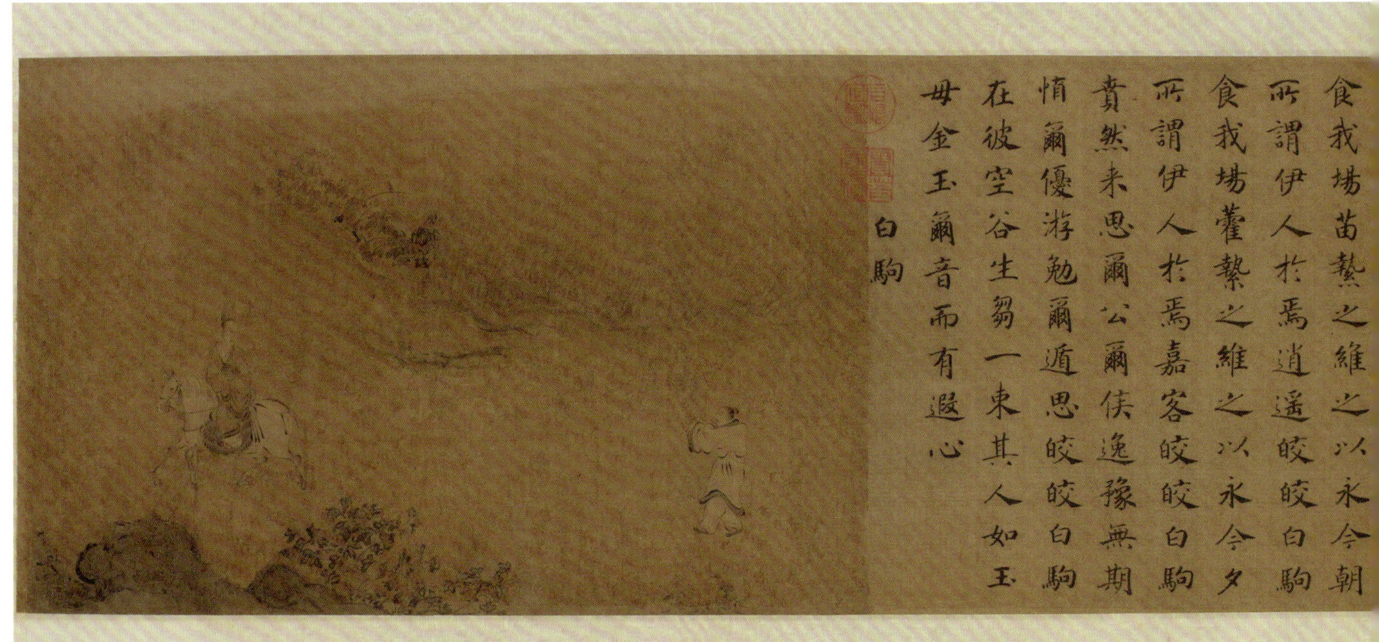
食我場苗縶之維之以永今朝
所謂伊人扵焉逍遙皎皎白駒
食我場藿縶之維之以永今夕
所謂伊人扵焉嘉客皎皎白駒
賁然来思爾公爾侯逸豫無期
慎爾優游勉爾遁思皎皎白駒
在彼空谷生芻一束其人如玉
毋金玉爾音而有遐心
白駒

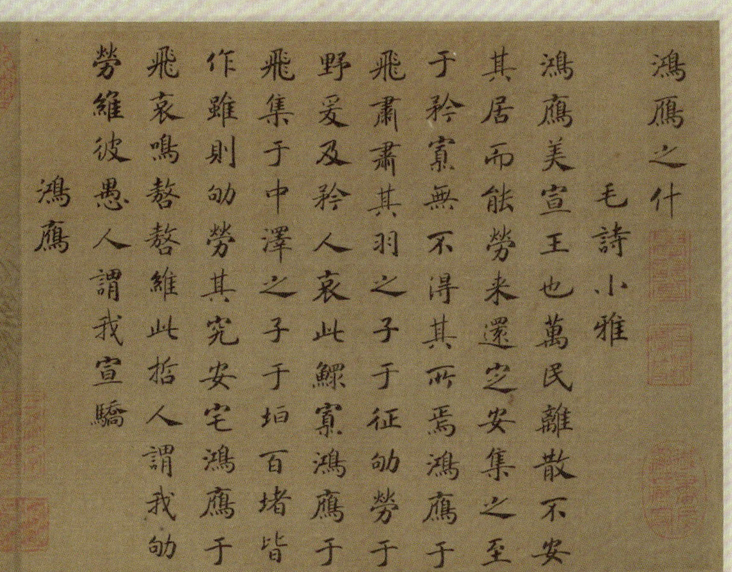

75. 诗经·小雅·鸿雁图

Illustrations of "Wild Geese" from Odes of Bin

南宋
（传）马和之
绢本设色
手卷
纵32.4、横1304.9厘米
大都会艺术博物馆

Southern Song dynasty (1127–1279)
Attributed to Ma Hezhi
Ink and color on silk
Handscroll
H×W : 32.4×1304.9 cm
The Metropolitan Museum of Art
Edward Elliott Family Collection, Gift of Douglas Dillon, 1984

我行其野刺宣王也我行其野蔽芾其樗昏姻之故言就爾居爾不我畜復我邦家我行其野言采其蓫昏姻之故言就爾宿爾不我畜言歸斯復我行其野言采其葍不思舊姻求爾新特成不以富亦祇以異
我行其野

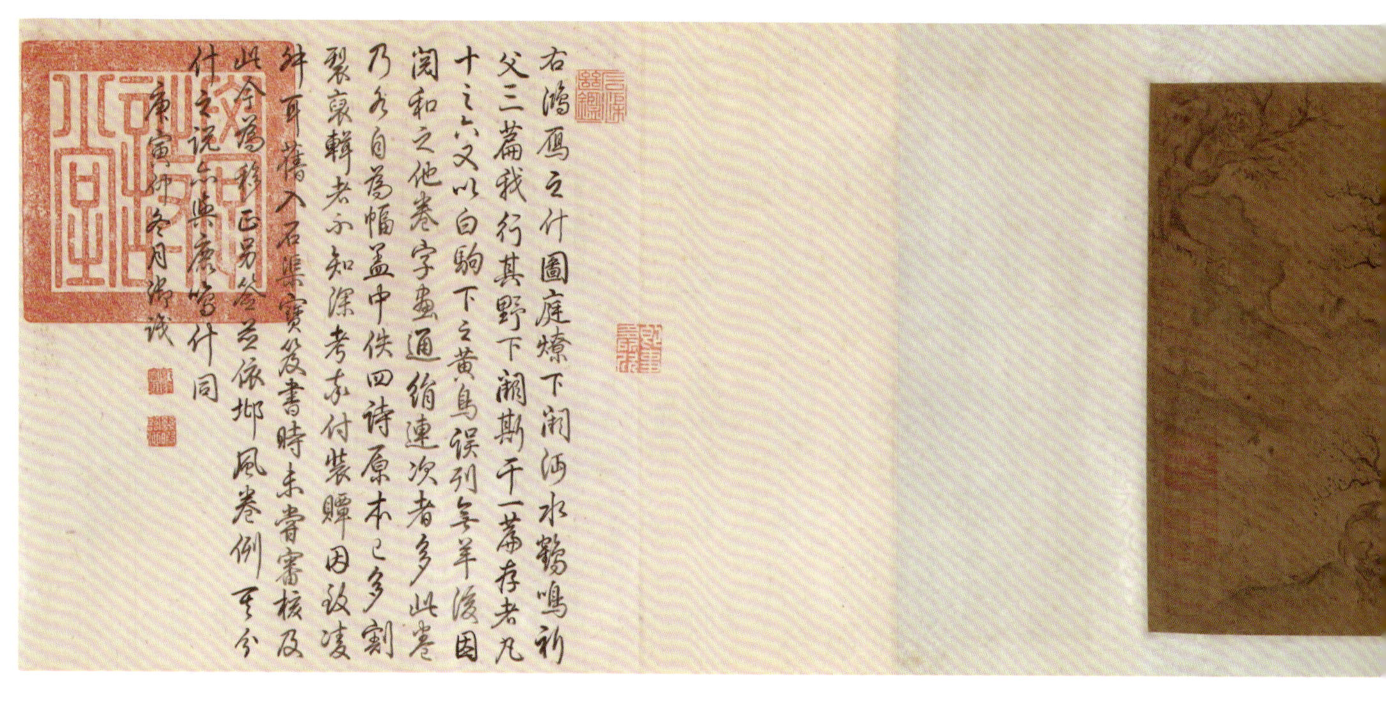

黃鳥刺宣王也黃鳥黃鳥無集于
穀無啄我粟此邦之人不我肯穀
言旋言歸復我邦族黃鳥黃鳥無
集于桑無啄我梁此邦之人不可
與明言旋言歸復我諸兄黃鳥黃
鳥無集于栩無啄我黍此邦之人
不可與處言旋言歸復我諸父
黃鳥

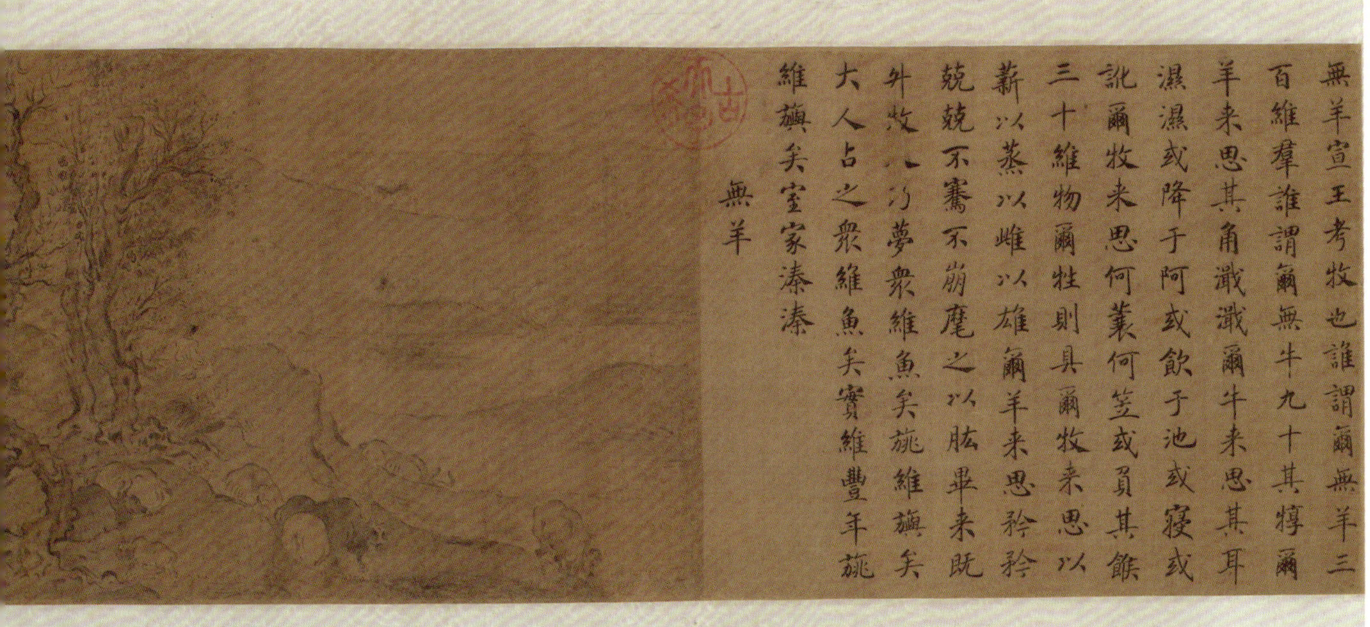
無羊宣王考牧也誰謂爾無羊三
百維羣誰謂爾無牛九十其犉爾
羊來思其角濈濈爾牛來思其耳
濕濕或降于阿或飲于池或寢或
訛爾牧來思何蓑何笠或負其餱
三十維物爾牲則具爾牧來思以
薪以蒸以雌以雄爾羊來思矜矜
兢兢不騫不崩麾之以肱畢來既
升牧人乃夢衆維魚矣旐維旟矣
大人占之衆維魚矣實維豐年旐
維旟矣室家溱溱
無羊

76. 秋郊牧牛图

南宋
（传）阎次平
绢本设色
册页
纵23、横21厘米
克利夫兰美术馆

Buffalo and Boy in Autumnal Landscape

Southern Song dynasty (1127–1279)
Attributed to Yan Ciping
Ink and color on silk
Album leaf
H×W : 23×21 cm
The Cleveland Museum of Art
Bequest of Mrs. A. Dean Perry 1997.86

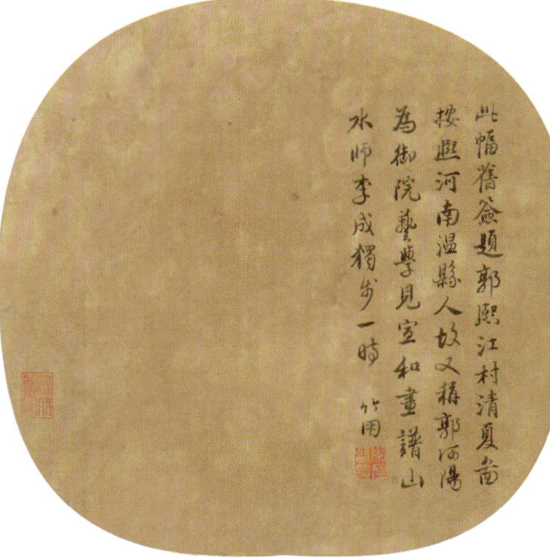

77. 松壑隐栖图

Hermitage by Pine-covered Bluff

南宋
（传）阎次于
绢本设色
册页
纵21.4、横23厘米
大都会艺术博物馆

Southern Song dynasty (1127–1279)
Attributed to Yan Ciyu
Ink and color on silk
Album leaf
H×W : 21.4×23 cm
The Metropolitan Museum of Art
Ex coll.: C. C. Wang Family, Purchase, Gift of Mr. and Mrs. Jeremiah Milbank and Gift of Mary Phelps Smith, in memory of Howard Caswell Smith, by exchange, 1973

版权支持

（按中文馆名音序排列）

鲍尔基金会鲍氏东方艺术馆
贝纳基博物馆
波士顿艺术博物馆
不列颠博物馆
大阪市立东洋陶瓷美术馆
大阪市立美术馆
大都会艺术博物馆
东京国立博物馆
费城艺术博物馆
菲尔德博物馆
弗利尔美术馆
弗利尔与赛克勒美术馆
哈佛艺术博物馆
荷兰国立博物馆
集美博物馆
金贝尔艺术博物馆
凯布朗利博物馆
克利夫兰艺术博物馆
科隆东亚艺术博物馆
洛杉矶郡艺术博物馆
明尼阿波利斯美术馆
奈良国立博物馆
普林斯顿大学美术馆
赛克勒博物馆
赛克勒美术馆
圣路易斯艺术博物馆
维多利亚和阿尔伯特博物馆
新南威尔士州美术馆
辛辛那提艺术博物馆
亚洲文明博物馆
耶鲁大学艺术博物馆
印第安纳波利斯艺术博物馆
芝加哥艺术博物馆

Image Contributors

(In Chinese Pinyin Order)

The Baur Foundation, Museum of Far Eastern Art
The Benaki Museum
The Museum of Fine Arts, Boston
The British Museum
The Museum of Oriental Ceramics, Osaka
The Osaka City Museum of Fine Arts
The Metropolitan Museum of Art
The Tokyo National Museum
The Philadelphia Museum of Art
The Field Museum
The Freer Gallery of Art
The Freer and the Arthur M. Sackler Gallery
The Harvard Art Museums
The Rijksmuseum
The Guimet Museum
The Kimbell Art Museum
The Quai Branly Museum
The Cleveland Museum of Art
The Museum of East Asian Art, Cologne
The Los Angeles County Museum of Art
The Minneapolis Institute of Art
The Nara National Museum
The Princeton University Art Museum
The Arthur M. Sackler Museum
The Arthur M. Sackler Gallery
The Saint Louis Art Museum
The Victoria and Albert Museum
The Art Gallery of New South Wales
The Cincinnati Art Museum
The Asian Civilisations Museum
The Yale University Art Gallery
The Indianapolis Museum of Art
The Art Institute of Chicago

编辑、出版人员

总 策 划 马汝军 谢 刚
选题策划 孙志鹏
主任编辑 邹懿男
出版统筹 丁 宁

责任编辑 李文彧 林 琳
特约编辑 丁文文
编　　辑 陈 雯 张小君 汪 欣 孙立英 白华召 施 然 马 源
赵笑笑 刘 琦 黄 艳 王 萌 王颖洁 王宏亮 毕力格图
责任校对 刘 义
实习编辑 齐倩颖 潘泓瑾

英文翻译 丁文文 耿玮浩
英文审校 韩 华

装帧设计 冷暖儿
图文版式 魏 丹 杨 丹 阮鸽鸽
责任印制 韦 舰 李珊珊

Editorial Staff

Chief Publisher Ma Rujun Xie Gang

Publisher Sun Zhipeng

Editorial Director Zou Yinan

Publishing Coordinator Ding Ning

Editors-in-Charge Li Wenyu Lin Lin

Contributing Editor Ding Wenwen

Editors Chen Wen Zhang Xiaojun Wang Xin Sun Liying Bai Huazhao Shi Ran Ma Yuan Zhao Xiaoxiao Liu Qi Huang Yan Wang Meng Wang Yingjie Wang Hongliang Biligt

Responsible Proofreader Liu Yi

Interns Qi Qianying Pan Hongjin

English Translators Ding Wenwen Geng Weihao

English Proofreader Han Hua

Cover Designer Leng Nuaner

Layout Designers Wei Dan Yang Dan Ruan Gege

Responsible Printing Coordinators Wei Jian Li Shanshan